Atchison, Eshelman

Los Angeles then and now

Atchison, Eshelman
Los Angeles then and now
ISBN/EAN: 9783744737609

Printed in Europe, USA, Canada, Australia, Japan

Cover: Foto ©ninafisch / pixelio.de

More available books at **www.hansebooks.com**

BY

ATCHISON & ESHELMAN
(HISTORIANS, ETC.)

ILLUSTRATED

LOS ANGELES:
PRESS GEO. RICE & SONS (INC.)
1897

PROLEGOMENA

ALMIGHTY truth, coupled with admiration for the onward strides of the metropolis, which sits at the foot of the majestic Sierra Madre *montana*, exhilarating with her genial climatic munificence all who come within its range, is the plea for this souvenir.

The aim has not been so much to illustrate as to point out the widely-extended possibilities of Los Angeles from a commercial and manufacturing aspect, recognizing the great truth that legitimate industries ever lie at the base of trade supremacy.

An intelligent and conservative consideration of the best means of expanding traffic tends to induce careful, practical men to thoroughly investigate the opportunities for profitable investments of capital. To this purpose "Los Angeles Then and Now" is partial, fully realizing that the only correct and successful basis of permanent and gratifying growth is strict adherence to sound business principles.

ONE OF OUR LOVELY HOMES Permission of R. J. Waters

THEN.

THE BEGINNING.

THE seed precedes the plant, the shrub the tree no less certainly than the discovery and the peopling lead the expansion and high estate of country and city. Equally true it is that in California, with her 151,801 square miles, pastoralism and cross-bearing joined hands in removing obstructions for the advancing culture and civilization.

Generations have rapidly passed from feudalism and knight-errantry into the realm of moral, mental and material felicity, studying ways and means to remove obstructional ignorance and discovering eternal principles and applying them to the up-lifting of mankind. In this evolutionary process the cross has not necessarily suffered. Its interests have been especially promoted by enlarged liberties and judicious protection.

THE FIRST COMERS.

The annals of events which transpired under Spanish authority in the settlement of California are not interwoven with the very warp of details. It is a question of any recordal warp.

RESIDENCE OF A. M. OZMAN

In 1602 the Spanish admiral, Vizcaino, sailed into San Diego Bay and noted its boundaries. One hundred and sixty-five years later another citizen of Spain, Father Junipero Serra, fitted out an expedition in Lower California, divided it into four parts, two going by land and two by sea, for Upper or Alta California.

Junipero Serra accompanied one of the parties by land. His lieutenant in things temporal was Galvez who thoughtfully carried with the enterprise two hundred head of cattle and a large variety of seeds and cuttings. From the latter sprang many of the beautiful flowers, palms, and other semi-tropic flora which now shed their beneficence on thousands of California homes.

The two vessels of Junipero Serra sailed into San Diego Bay, April 11, 1767, and the union of the land and sea forces became the nucleus at that point of a new civilization for the aborigines. This scheme of improvement contemplated the cross for its center and territorial expansion for its circumference. California became the child of Spain and the Indians, whether voluntarily or otherwise the unrecorded events deponeth not, became neophytes of the cross.

Evidences, however, are not wanting as to the unselfish and emendatory conation of the pioneer civilizers, who, up to the close of the last century, strove to elevate the minds and hearts of the natives rather than seek pecuniary advantages for themselves. Doubtless these removers of obstructions in the interests of a higher civiliza-

OUR HANDSOME COURTHOUSE.

tion preferred to be called the Sons of Pharoah's daughter rather than enjoy the pleasures of selfish greed for a season.

The death of Junipero Serra and his associates was the ushering in of selfish and personal exaltation, which, in time, degrades, banishing the practical and imperishable principle of seeking the welfare of others. Such a condition could not otherwise than produce a decline of the Indian race. Unable to resist the ravages of selfishness, the red man gradually disappeared, so that now there is but a remnant,—a handful of aimless, listless beings, the tailings of the high purpose and extraordinary efforts of the Padres to eliminate low conditions and transfer into a better and nobler state. Thus the California Indians have gone through every grade of experience except that of *abiding*.

EXTENSIONS.

Soon after the founding of the San Diego Mission, the promoters of Spanish interests pushed their way northward and arriving at a river, whose source is in the Sierra Madre mountains, named it San Gabriel, in honor of the Angel Gabriel. Here a mission was planted, but in September, 1771, it was moved to the point where it now is, near Alhambra.

PROSPERITY.

The rich soil, perfect climatic conditions, and abundance of water with frugal management, enabled the Padres to gather wheat, and cattle, and sheep, and goats, and horses in plentitude.

Permission of HOTEL DEL CORONADO

The business interests, as well as the spiritual beneficences, were managed by the Fathers, and so successful were they in temporal accretions that in 1825 the value of the live stock was $8,850,000; church ornaments and money, $1,500,000, or a total of $10,350,000. Nine years later, 1834, there were 66,345 horses, 1,044,470 head of cattle and a large number of sheep and o'her domestic animals, grazing on the hills and in the valleys—a vast pastoral domain uninvaded by the hum of industry's wheel, yet paving the way for the *Now*.

DATE PALM Permission of Hotel Del Coronado

LOS ANGELES.

NEUSTRA Señora la Reina de Los Angeles (Loce-ang-he les) was first settled by twelve familes of mixed people who came from Senora, Mexico. They were not possessed with an insatiable desire to know and understand the source and relations of the fundamental law of things, but were wholly dependent upon the intelligent class for subsistence. Their dwellings were made of adobe covered with brea found near their habitations. In 1790 the population numbered 140. In 1800 it amounted to 315 whites. In 1809 Samuel Workman was the first American to arrive. The development was slow. Education did not find favorable admittance until 1817, when the first school was opened. In 1822 the first town council was organized. The old church near the Plaza was completed.

THE CAPITAL.

In 1835 the Mexican Congress passed an act designating Los Angeles as the capital of Alta California; but Monterey disputed this edict and effort and retained the seat of government until Pio Pico became governor in 1846, when the first,

R. W. BURNHAM

and, what proved to be the last, session was held here, the United States coming into possession of the territory in 1847.

SANTA FE TRAIL.

During 1835 the great Santa Fe trail came into existence, thus establishing connection between Santa Fe, New Mexico, and Alta California points. By 1846 the trail had gained some overland traffic, hides and tallow going eastward and a few articles of manufactured goods coming westward. These might be termed the "seeds" of the present "Santa Fe" traffic.

CHANGE OF GOVERNMENT.

Spain may be said to have been a leader in territorial acquisition during the sixteenth, seventeenth and eighteenth centuries, but her methods of colonization and perpetuation are extraordinary only in decay. In Alta California, as elsewhere in her dependencies, the obtaining of revenue was the prime consideration. Nourishing and developing Alta California was not a part of Spanish policy. Her soldiery was recruited from the criminal class. They were poorly fed, rarely paid and illy provided. This condition was not fruitful of patriotism; hence when Commodore Stockton and General Fremont resolved to possess the land in the name of the United States in 1846, the difficulties readily vanished. Gen. Kearney arriving at the close of the year, his forces and Commodore Stockton's were united and on January 10, 1847, Los Angeles passed into their possession and the change of government brought about improved commercial conditions.

GOLDEN CRESTED.

In 1849 the discovery of gold changed the entire aspect of affairs, since which time California may well be denominated golden-crested; for this addition of wealth-getting to her flocks and herds, and the subsequent cereal and fruit productions, have placed her in the foremost ranks of affluence. All her developments and opulence are golden-hued with high attainments. The population of Los Angeles at this time was 2500.

FIRST OVERLAND STAGE-COACH.

October 7, 1858, the first overland coach by way of the Texas Staked Plains through El Paso and Yuma arrived. Thus the ploughshare of overland transportation made its first furrow in the native glebe and became the heralder of a coming enormous traffic.

ARRIVAL OF TELEGRAPHY.

October 3d, 1860, the small, sharp noise of the telegraph was first heard in the city of Angels. This was an additional evidence of the arrival of new conditions and the waning of the old. The discovery of gold, the production of wheat and cattle, the incursions of the invincible Saxons who speedily opened up transportation facilities by sea and land stimulated trade and brought prosperity with great rapidity.

LOS ANGELES: THEN AND NOW

RESIDENCE OF E. C. SCHNABEL

FIRST RAILROAD.

The first railroad into the city was built by the people. The county issued bonds to the amount of $225,000, and built a road therewith to Wilmington, San Pedro Harbor. The eyes of the people have not ceased looking at San Pedro harbor as the natural gateway of the coming oriental commerce. October 6th, 1869, marked the completion of the people's railway. The natives were astounded on seeing a locomotive and cars speeding over the country. Admiring the simplicity of their fathers and dreading the terrors of innovations, they clung, with tenacity, to their wooden-wheeled carretos, their wooden plows, ox yokes, and rawhide. The iron age had not come to them. That which they needed they made. Rawhide served instead of nails, and screws and bolts and hinges. Nature's inswinging and outswinging door was ever open to them. The Mestizo is always Spanish; hence mix the blood as you will, the Moorish comes to the top. Their industry was mixed with uncomplaining qualities, their habits and customs having been hewn out of a pastoral and patriarchal life. The age of steel, if not *steal*, has well-nigh rooted them all out. The iron horse did its share.

THE FIRST FINE FABRIC.

The Pico block, corner of Main street and the Plaza, rose into magnificence in 1869, and was utilized for business and a hotel. Thirty years have not yet fled into the unreturning time, yet

FRANK G. SCHUMACHER

scores of structures have overshadowed the Pico. In its day it was pre-eminently a leader, and as the city takes on age perhaps even the Pico House may be permitted to enlist in the ranks of the Landmark Club.

THE INITIAL BANKS.

Exclusive ruralism was now giving place to manufacturing and commerce. Trade relations were established and a bank became a necessity; hence, in 1869, Governor Downey opened one in the Downey block. This was soon followed by the Farmers' and Merchants' bank under the direction of I. W. Hellman and others. The modern American had come. He came planting. His plants were carefully watered and cultivated. They accreted. They abide.

MORE STAGE LINES.

Connections with San Diego, Havilah, San Bernardino and San Francisco were established by means of omnibuses. The Concord stage supplanted the caballero. Six or ten might ride instead of one.

RAILROADS.

The Southern Pacific Company was an early arrival and has proven a persevering stayer, first securing the people's railway to San Pedro, and then obtaining control of the Santa Monica line which had been built by Tom Scott. September 8, 1877, this company made connections with its Central Pacific line in San Francisco, this giving Los Angeles an all-rail route eastward.

From 1875 to 1882 the wheels of commerce revolved slowly, trade conditions were very unsatisfactory, the people were inclined to restlesness, many desiring to rid themselves of their holdings and seek more remunerative investments elsewhere. In the latter year, however, the Southern Pacific Company completed its track to the Mexican Gulf ports and the fleet-footed, lustre-eyed gazelle of prosperity, bounding once more over city and country, causing charming cheerfulness to possess the minds and hearts of the people, the population leaping from 33,881 in 1880 to over 51,000 in 1890.

November 9, 1885, a new transcontinental highway of commerce, the Santa Fe Railway, gained entrance into the city. This was the signal for sharp, stimulating competition in transmissional trade, thus quickening every branch of business. The years 1886-87 witnessed phenomenal commercial transactions. Rate cutting between competing railway lines resulted in bringing many thousands of passengers from Missouri River points at $5 each. The city and country became a vast bee-hive of humanity, not, however, seeking the honey of permanent prosperity by sound industrial means, but by transferrance one from the other. Climatic elements so genial and full of blessings to mankind, unsurpassed mountain seenery, the almost limitless variety of soil productions, the close proximity of the mighty Pacific, whose broad bosom beckons a sure and growing oriental commerce—all these doubtle

created unparelled enthusiasm in the minds of the newcomers. The ready real estate promoter was at hand. He always is. His quick preception marshalled the necessary forces to rush sales. The country was surveyed and staked into lots, varying in size from 25x150 feet to 50x200 feet. A day was set in which to offer them to investors. Train loads of men and women, accompanied by the auctioneer and brass band proceeded to the city on paper. Arriving, the auctioneer spread his map on the ground, put his foot on it to keep it from the playful antics of the sea breeze, he generously offered the lots which went quickly at prices ranging from $200 to $1200 each. Millions of dollars were thus invested; massive hotels sprung up in every village, water works were constructed, white tents, resembling the encampment of vast soldiery graced the lots, thus signifying that the multitude really believed that if they had not found the fount of perpetual youth, they had had at least discerned the region of continuous joy. In this their conclusions were not far removed from the facts, but they soon learned that the lasting delights come only by a strict observance of the laws of practical industry.

ISOTHERMAL CONDITIONS.

It is a well-established law that where conditions exist which resulted in building up great cities that similar influences elsewhere must result, when discovered and observed by thoughtful, practical men, in like accretions of wealth. The isothermal actuation existing where man has attained to, and maintained the highest, moral, intellectual and commercial attitudes, will enable man to do the same thing under life influences. The mean temperature of 60 degrees F. characterized the regions of Babalon, Athens, Sparta, Rome and other eastern cities where thought-conceptions stand pre-eminent among mankind.

Coming to our own continent, the isothermal line of 60 degrees mean temperature, beginning near New York, extends west through Philadelphia, St. Louis, Kansas City to Los Angeles, holding within its reach Chicago, Omaha, Denver and San Francisco. This mean temperature of 60 degrees F. wherein the human race reaches and maintains its highest development, may account, to some extent, for the phenomenal growth of Los Angeles and surroundings. Surely the marvelous beauties and unbounded productions of California are just so many proofs that almighty truth and fixed elementary principles are the six-winged seraphim whose flights dispel error and mischievous, hurtful hindrances.

HENNE BUILDING

NOW

EMERGING from her baptism of over-speculation in 1887, Los Angeles maintained, in a remarkable manner, her position as a veritable giant in the southwest. Notwithstanding the reactionary influences which everywhere encircled her, the population increased from 51,000 in 1890, to 103,000 in 1897, or a gain of over 100 per cent. in seven years. The inspiration of Chicago is upon her.

Then the city was destitute of a single paved street. *Now* there are to her credit nearly two hundred miles of graded and graveled streets; fourteen miles of paved highways, and one hundred and thirty-five miles of cement and asphalt footways, and nearly one hundred and forty miles of sewer. An outfall sewer eighteen miles in length reaches the ocean.

WATER SUPPLY.

The city is supplied with an abundance of water, which has its source in the snowy peaks of the Sierra Madre range.

RAPID TRANSIT.

Less than fifteen years ago the city had one

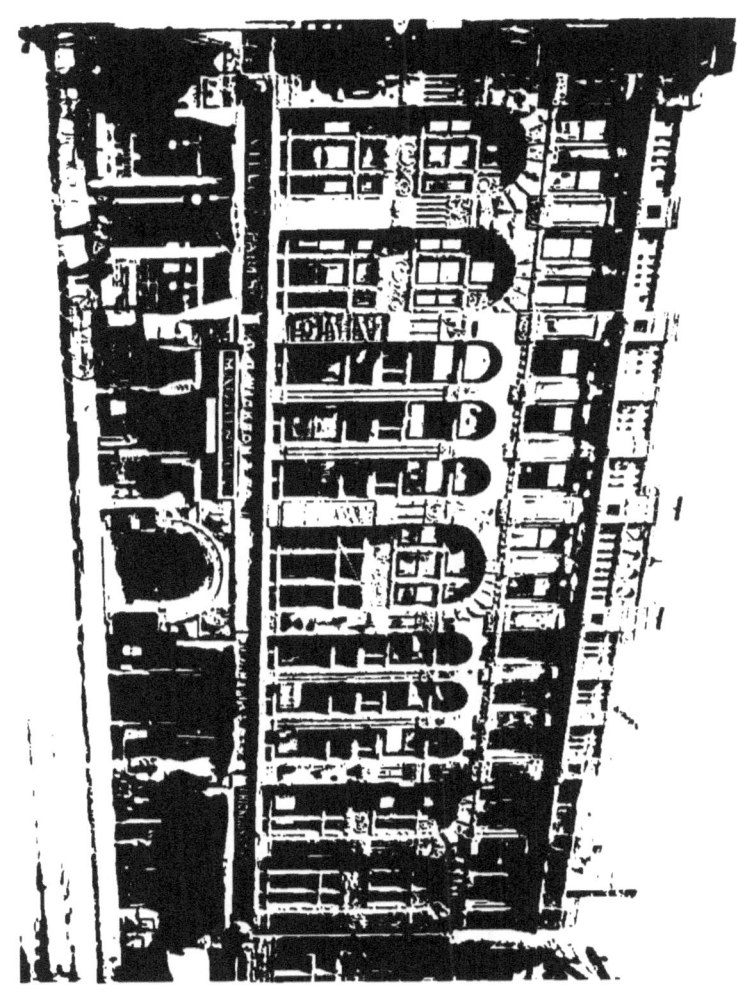

POTOMAC BUILDING

horse-car line. Now the total mileage is one hundred and twenty-seven, ninety eight per cent. of which is operated by electricity. The three well equipped systems traverse a wide area, reaching all parts of the city. The local electric line reaches Mt. Lowe via Pasadena and Altadena to the north, and Santa Monica by the sea on the west. Handsome and well-equipped cars leave the central part of the city hourly for those points, the routes passing amidst ever-changing, enchanting rural and mountain scenery. Breakfasting by the seaside, you may leave the cornfields at Santa Monica, view the deciduous fruit orchards, the orange and lemon groves on the way to Los Angeles, admire the stately hills of Highland, enjoy lovely Pasadena and meek Altadena, wonder at Rubio canyon, elevate your soul on the Incline railway, esteem the wonders beneath you on Echo mountain, and shout in ecstacy of delight at Alpine Tavern, 5000 feet above the ocean, lunch, and return to the sea to behold the setting sun in the mirrored waters.

TRANSPORTATION FACILITIES.

In addition to the most excellent rapid transit in the city, there are twelve lines of railway, like the spokes of a wheel, radiating from the city. To the north extends the Southern Pacific to Portland via San Francisco. Also to Santa Barbara, where connections with the coast line will soon be effected. The Terminal reaches out to Tropico and Glendale, westward by the Southern Pacific and by the Santa Fe to Santa

UNIVERSITY OF SOUTHERN CALIFORNIA

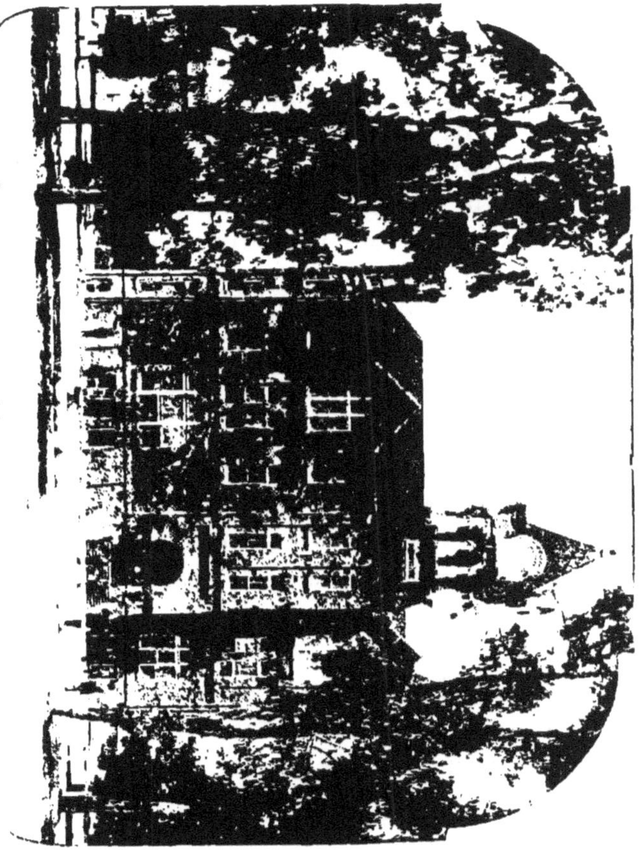

Monica. Redondo is reached by the Santa Fe and Redondo Beach railway. Southwest to San Pedro the Terminal and the Southern Pacific are operated. South the Santa Fe reaches San Diego and Santa Ana, and the Southern Pacific extends to Santa Ana and Tustin. Eastward up the great San Gabriel and San Bernardino valleys stretches the Southern Pacific on its way to New Orleans, while the Santa Fe, passing through the Cajon Pass, reaches on to Chicago The Santa Fe, through its Southern California division, captivates its patrons with its kite-shaped track, up the valleys, via Pasadena, Monrovia, Azusa, Lordsburg, North Ontario, Rialto, San Bernardino, Redlands, Colton, Riverside, Orange, Anaheim, Los Angeles.

These Transcontinental systems now bring eastern cities and trade points into close touch with Los Angeles, and the fourth one via Salt Lake City will doubtless soon materialize, since there are yet only 300 miles to construct.

SEAWARD.

Great and helpful as these transcontinental systems are, the sea route is destined to become equally wonderful and beneficial. South America, the Pacific islands, Japan and China have caught the traffic inspiration, and Los Angeles is sure to secure a share of the results.

COMMERCIAL BODIES.

For the betterment of home and international trade relations and the material development of the city there exist the Chamber of Commerce,

Permission of HOTEL DEL CORONADO

the Board of Trade and the Merchants' and Manufacturers' Association. Ever watchful to foster and encourage the exchange of products with countries that can supply us with what cannot be grown here, and to promote the substantial growth of the city and country, these commercial associations are truly the heart-pulses of the metropolis.

These business bodies will meet you at the threshold of the city or at the gateway to Southern California and give you substantial aid and encouragement. There will be no absurd offer of a bonus or anything that savors of corrupt practices, but if the opening is here for your consideration and you see it to your advantage rest assured a welcome that will please, a hospitality magnetic in its influence and the incentive that a broad and liberal business man can becomingly accord another, awaits you.

RELIGIOUS AND BENEVOLENT.

In the interests of religion there are about one hundred churches, and devoted to charitable work are the Associated Charities, the Children's Home Society, The Florence Home, The Newsboys' Home, The Sisters' School and Orphan Asylum, The Los Angeles Orphans' Home and Hollenbeck Home.

EDUCATIONAL.

It is with becoming pleasure that we present the following scholarly review of the educational interests from the pen of President G. W. White, D. D., of the Southern California University:

ELLEN BEACH YAW   Permission of Marceau

HIGHER EDUCATION.

BY GEO. W. WHITE, D. D., PRESIDENT OF THE UNIVERSITY OF SOUTHERN CALIFORNIA.

PERHAPS no one item would be of more importance to many people contemplating removal to Los Angeles, than the facilities for the higher education of their children.

As in others, so in this important matter, the city is able to afford first-class advantages. The growth of the institutions for higher education, while perhaps not equal in proportion to the city's rapid development, has been very marked and gratifying. While these institutions have been mainly denominational in control, as are the great majority of the colleges and universities of this country, they have not been narrowly sectarian in character

St. Vincent's college, under the control of the Catholic church, was, perhaps, the first college established in the city, having its buildings located at a point which seemed then quite removed from the business part of the city. But in the rapid development of the city from 1885 to 1888, they soon found the business houses crowding close up to them, so they sold their location on Hill between Sixth and Seventh, and removed to the corner of Grand avenue and Washington, where they now have ample and beautiful grounds, a commodious building, with a large church adjacent, and a strong, well-equipped school.

The Dunkard's have a large colony at Lordsburg, about 25 miles east of Los Angeles, and founded a college there in 1888. It is thriving under their careful management.

The Baptist people located a college in the beautiful section west of Westlake Park, about 1886, but on account of some financial misfortunes with their property, have only been able to maintain it as an academy. However, they have developed it into a military academy, making it the only school of this character in the city. It thus has a peculiar field to itself. It is a boarding school, and is well managed. Walter R. Wheat is principal.

The Presbyterian church established their school, Occidental College, originally, just outside the city limits, below Boyle Heights, where it was making good growth and a good record, but had the misfortune to have its building destroyed by fire in 1895. The school was then located in the old St. Vincent's College building on Hill street, where it has since remained. A new site, at Highland Park, midway between Los Angeles and Pasadena, has now been secured, and a fund raised for a new building

BEACH VIEW

Permission Hotel Del Coronado

which is soon to be erected. Rev. Guy W. Wadsworth is President.

At Pasadena, ten miles from Los Angeles, is located the Throop Polytechnic Institute, an institution for academic and industrial education. It is well-equipped, especially for teaching the industrial sciences, and is doing a fine grade of work. Dr. Walter A. Edwards is the President. It was founded in 1888.

The Congregational Church has no school in Los Angeles, but has a very excellent one, Pomona College, founded in 1887, at Claremont, about 30 miles east of Los Angeles. They have good buildings, in a beautiful location. An endownment fund of $100,000 has recently been pledged. Prof. E. C. Norton is Dean.

The only university in Southern California is located in Los Angeles, but its incorporate name, the University of Southern California, indicates that it does not plan to confine its field to the city alone. In fact its original plan involved the establishment of separate colleges at several different places in the southern end of the State. It was founded in 1880, by the Methodist Episcopal Church, and had at that time only one department, a college of Letters, located in Los Angeles. In 1887, under the influence of the marvelous development of the city and country at this time in progress, the institution was expanded into University proportion—colleges of Theology and Medicine being opened, the former at San Fernando, the latter at Los Angeles, while plans

EASTLAKE PARK   Permission of "Greater Los Angeles"

were made for a college of Fine Arts at San Diego and a portion of the buildings were erected. A fine Seminary building was erected at Escondido, and an Agricultural College had already been opened at Ontario. Lands were donated to these different schools at that time for buildings and endowment, sufficient to give, according to the inflated values of that date, an aggregate value of more than two million dollars. Of course great things were expected of the institution from this promising beginning; but the collapse of the "boom" soon effected great changes. Values of the landed endowments rapidly declined, and much property was lost from inability to meet the conditions of the bequests. However, by wise and prompt efforts to meet these changed conditions, the institution has come out of its crisis with a splendid property still remaining. Deeds of trust have been changed to suit the new conditions; a plan of concentrating all the schools in Los Angeles, to mutually support each other, is being rapidly consummated. For a few years, while these readjustments were in progress, the institution had only small available resources, and the work suffered in consequence. But within the last three years, since the adjustments were completed, strong efforts, with marked success, have been made to build up the school. Almost entirely new equipment has been put in, especially in science lines, until now the extensive laboratories compare favorably with those of much more pretentious institutions, and its science

LOS ANGELES; THEN AND NOW 47

Permission of HOTEL DEL CORONADO

work, under expert professors, is accepted in the best institutions of the land; cuts of some of these equipments are embodied in this sketch.

It now has the following departments in active operation, with a faculty of more than 60 professors, all told: Colleges of Liberal Arts, Theology, Medicine, Dentistry and Music, together with schools of Art and Elocution, and a preparatory school. There were in all departments last year, over 500 students, and the grade of work done is very high. The faculty has been very carefully selected. Every professor has had special collegiate and graduate training for his particular line in the best institutions of this country. Some have also had the advantage of studying in the Universities abroad. It is the aim of the institution to give strictly first-class work on as low a tuition rate as is possible. Its courses are modern and broad, giving a wide range of electives, including a strong course in Pedagogy. While it is a church school, and insists on earnest moral influences, it does not permit narrow bigotry and sectarianism. Its faculty is made up from all the leading religious denominations, and it gives to the children of all evangelical ministers, as well as to all candidates for the ministry and missionary work of all such churches, half rates of tuition, just the same as to those of the Methodist faith. Geo. W. White, D. D., is President.

Besides these schools of Collegiate and University grade, there are quite a number of private

MILO M. POTTER

schools giving preparatory work. There are also two flourishing business colleges beside several private schools of Art, Music and Elocution. In addition, the largest State Normal School of the State is located in Los Angeles. Edwin T. Pierce is principal. Thus it may be seen that coupled with its exceptionally fine climate, Los Angeles has educational advantages of a high order to offer.

THE NEW PALESTINE.*

FROM one of the numerous valuable, readable and interesting pamphlets issued by the Chamber of Commerce, we clip the following:

"Southern California is frequently likened to Italy, but Palestine furnishes a more appropriate comparison. Like Palestine, Southern California is a long, narrow strip of land, bounded on the west by a summer sea, and on the east by mountains, snow-clad during a portion of the year; like Palestine, Southern California has a dry, equitable climate; like Palestine, Southern California is a land of the olive and the vine, a land where every man "may sit under his own fig tree"; a land "flowing with milk and honey." Unlike Palestine, however, Southern California is not a melancholy reminder of its former greatness, but a center of active, aggressive American enterprise; a region in which the best thought and energy of the American people are finding their crowning development, under the most genial clime in which the Anglo-Saxon race ever wooed the favors of Mother Earth.

"The seven southern counties of Southern

LOS ANGELES: THEN AND NOW

Permission of HOTEL REDONDO

California, namely, Los Angeles, Orange, San Bernardino, Riverside, San Diego, Ventura and Santa Barbara, with a shore line of 275 miles, embrace an area of nearly 45,000 square miles, or 30 per cent of the area of the State. This is an area as large as Pennsylvania, and a little smaller than England. The population, in 1880 was 64,371, or 7½ per cent of the population of the State. In 1890 it was 201,352, or 16⅔ of the population of the State. Today it is over 300,000, or more than 20 per cent of the population of the State.

"Notwithstanding this remarkably rapid growth, it will be many years before Southern California is overcrowded Greece, with a little over half the area, has twelve times the population of Southern California; Switzerland, with one-third the area, has sixteen times the population, and Portugal, with three-fourths the area, has twenty-five times the population. These, also, are mountainous countries, and largely dependent upon hroticulture and agriculture for support."

PUBLIC BUILDINGS.

Los Angeles is graced with as fine a court house and jail, on a beautiful elevation, as can be found anywhere, and the city hall on Broadway, the city jail on West First street, are model structures. The grand public library is an honorable monument to the intellectual greatness of her people.

H. W. CHASE

PARKS⚜

Ten parks afford animating delightful outdoor resorts for all classes; and where three hundred and fifty days in the year are adorned with the genial rays of the sun and atmospheric conditions beckon to its pleasurable influences, these parks are scenes of multitudes of inspired folk. When Elysian park, with its hundreds of acres of hills and vales shall have been turned into one vast arboretum, where the flora peculiar to California—her magnificent trees, and almost endless variety of plants and flowers—shall attract botanists from all parts of America, then shall Los Angeles more than ever realize the unnumbered blessings set about and in the midst of her. And when the munificent gift of 3,000 acres to the city by Mr. Griffith J. Griffith shall take on boulevards, lawns, flowers, lakes, and the fauna needful for its perfect adornment, then shall Los Angeles lead the cities of the earth in her unexcelled out-door attractions.

POWER AND LIGHTING⚜

The grand and stately mountains, rising above the clouds at the back-ground of our cities and unsurpassed rural districts, do not simply render service in modifying air-currents and collecting and sending down the blessings of waters, but their elevations are being utilized for power, light and heating purposes. The waters of the San Gabriel and Santa Ana rivers are being harnessed to dynamos which will send forth many thousand horse-power for power, lighting and heating purposes in Los Angeles and other cities. The erection of a building in this city with the necessary power and lighting facilities to assist men of small capital to manufacture, would be met with hearty response. This power conveyed to small rooms where the busy artisan can make something more than tracks, will add very materially to the expansion of trade and manufacturing. For other useful and remunerative fields for manufacturing investments, the reader is referred to the views of leading business men of the city.

PACKING HOUSES.

As a source of trade, there are not only establishments in which oranges by the trainload, and lemons, dried fruits, nuts and cereals are collected and forwarded to inviting homes and foreign markets, but the Cudahy packing house has given a gratifying impetus to hog raising in the corn and alfalfa regions, where swine can be fed on green food every month in the year, and the general weather conditions enables them to mature much quicker than in rigorous and changeable climates.

RECREATION.

There are few places on this mundane sphere that excel California in natural attractions and diversity of fascinations. The near-by mountains awe one with their stateliness; and the numerous peaks and cañons and nooks and waterfalls, per-

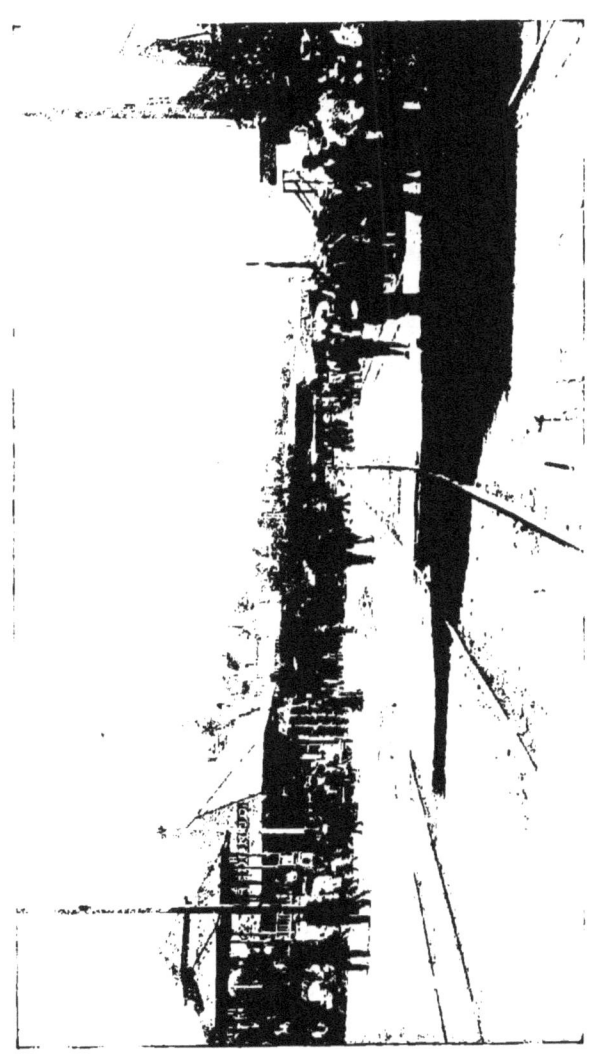

Permission of HOTEL REDONDO

fectly ozoned, inspire with their wild flowers, ferns, and multitudinous charms. To camp amidst these is to enjoy all that is possible in a partnership with unsullied nature.

Seaward, the briny deep no less generously bestows its captivating recreations. Here tired nature seeks her ease and lavatory longings, and is admiringly gratified. Here the angler can pursue his profession to the delight of his aspirations, and the satisfaction of his keenest appetite; for the mighty Pacific is replete with the finest piscatorial creatures.

Or if the heart longs for the beautiful as well as the useful in flowers, plants and cereals, let it turn into the rural regions all around this queen of the angels and it will be ravished with the seemingly endless variety of roses, crysanthemums, verbenas, pinks, pansies, petunias, poppys, asters, asperneas, allyssum, zinneas, sweet peas, snap dragons, violets, lupins, larkspurs, nasturtiums, mignonettes, petunias, carnations, etc., palms, firs, pines, rubber trees, magnolias, peppers, camphors, cedars, centurys, giant cacti, and many other interesting shrubs; great stretches of wheat and barley, sugar beets and canaigre,— in short, in his perambulations the tourist, the investor or recreator can find all that is needful to enrapture and heighten the veriest dormant condition of his being. He needs no more.

And no less charming to the eye of culture are the vast stretches of vineyards, orange, lemon and deciduous orchards, whose perfect fruits

A. JACOBY

peep out from under and about the dark green foliage with a glow of grandeur and magnificence that silences pen and tongue in the effort to correctly portray. The artistic eye simply moves the tongue to exclaim, "Oh, wonderful!" and then drops into utter silence, realizing the paucity of language to express the varying, perfect colors in bloom, in leaf, in limb, in fruit mature and maturing. There is but one Southern California, and there could by no possibility be more than one, for there is this only nook on this great big round globe with sea and mountain, and soil, and water influences so admirably combined. One is enough! If you are not in this one, come into it now!

BANKING.

MR. R. J. WATERS, Vice-President of the citizens' Bank, and Director of the Columbia Savings Bank, when asked to give his opinion as to the financial condition of Southern California, stated that the outlook for this section was very encouraging.

Mr. Waters says "that in the varying fortunes of the people of California, there has been no one thing that has contributed more towards the prosperity and growth of the State, than the confidence inspired by the conduct of its banks. Especially is this the case in the Southern part of the State, where the main industries for the ten years last past have been almost entirely experimental.

"The solidity of its banking institutions has been to Southern California the ground-work and foundation for the faith which has buoyed up the toiling orchardist and farmer, and inspired to renewed effort the struggling merchant and manufacturer.

"There is no general rule but that has its exceptions, and consequently it is not to be expected that the banker of Southern California, as elsewhere, is exempt from the vicisitudes of all business transactions ; but in no location or State has there been less of actual mismanagement than here.

" It cannot be denied that amongst these exceptions there are cases of comparatively recent date, where the operations of so-called banking institutions have been of such a character as to merit the condemnation of all right-minded men engaged in promoting financial institutions, as well as the public at large. But these exceptions are comparatively few, and tend stronger to prove the rule and establish beyond question the high standing and sound conduct of the great majority of our financial houses, both State and National.

" It is not the province of an article of this length to furnish statistical information for public use, but as evidence of the growth of the banking business in California, it will perhaps be well to refer to Bank Commissioners' Report of September 1st, 1890, and September 1st, 1895, as

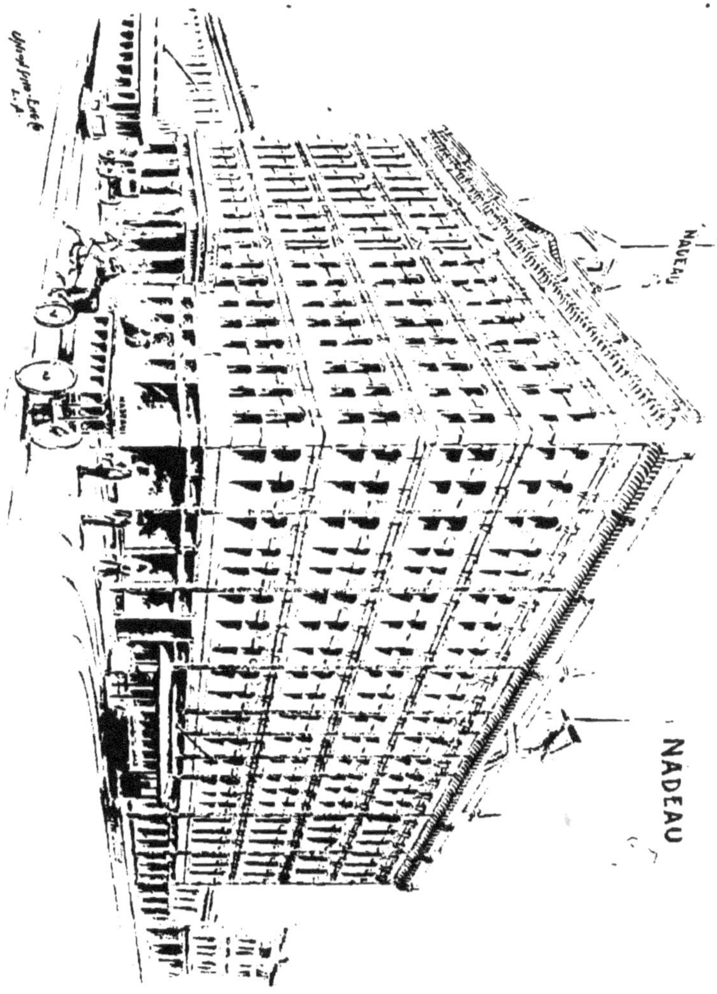

showing the healthy growth of financial institutions during this period.

"In the report of the State Banks to the Commissioners, of September 1st, 1890, the assets and liabilities were shown to be $113,015,-945.33, and in the report dated September 1st, 1895, the assets and liabilities were reported as $135,160,130.28, an increase of over $22,000,000.

"By comparison in report it will be seen that the Southern part of the State has kept pace with the Northern section.

"The report of the Savings Banks for 1890, shows assets and liabilities of $103,071,296.75; for 1895, $148,517,147.36, an increase of over $45,000,000. The same comparison as of Commercial banks will attest the healthy growth of Southern California Banks.

"Some portion of the increase above set forth may be due to the changing of private to State banks, but there is sufficient growth to denote a healthy condition of our finances, and to indicate that the conservatism of our bankers has not proved prejudicial to the banking business in this section.

"In the early days of State formation in the Western part of our Union, the history of banking was not such as to inspire confidence in the community, and the many failures of financial institutions at that time, created confusion and entailed great hardships, which in most cases continued for many years.

"Happily for us, no such condition confront-

Permission of HOTEL DEL CORONADO

ed us here to any marked degree, and we have been comparatively free from the ill effects arising therefrom.

"I think we are to be congratulated upon our good fortune in the possession of men of ability and integrity to conduct our financial institutions."

The above is certainly a credit to the city, and will doubtless be read with interest by every reader of "Los Angeles Then and Now."

THE MEDICAL PROFESSION.

THE MEDICAL FRATERNITY OF LOS ANGELES, IN COMPARISON WITH THAT OF OTHER CITIES OF THE SAME SIZE. BY D. W. EDLEMAN, A. B., M. D.

The Medical Fraternity of Los Angeles, including all who practice medicine here—of all schools or of no schools—will reach in number beyond four hundred. This means an average of one practitioner to each two hundred and fifty of the population; a proportion so large as to be unsurpassed, no doubt, in that respect by any city of equal size anywhere.

This is attributable to the fact that our mild climate calls from the severe summers and severer winters of the East many physicians as health seekers; and among these there are always some who are enticed by our sunshine to remain. The result is readily conceived: A medical fraternity replete with men whose ability and standing range from that designated "best in the

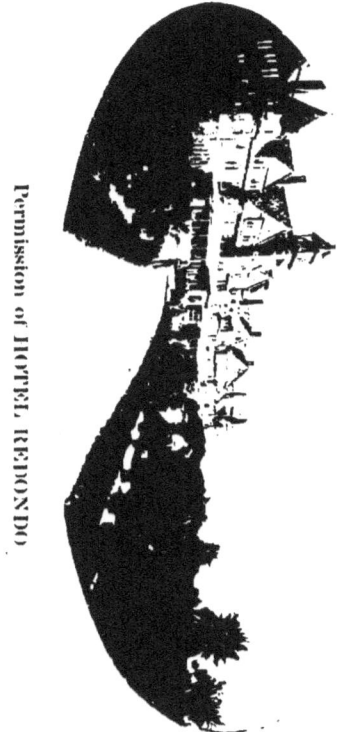

Permission of HOTEL REDONDO.

United States," to the very lowest of the worst quack-ridden city.

Though far from what are popularly understood to be the seats of scientific learning, Los Angeles with, and to a certain extent *because* of, its metropolitan population can claim, with justice, to have among its medical men surgeons as bold, and withal as skillful; physicians as well read, and as thoroughly able as any city of similar size in the world. They are drawn to Los Angeles from all countries, and were the better class alone to come, the medical profession here would be unsurpassed. But with the best have come also the worst; and as the city is peopled by many health seekers, the quacks, irregulars and incapables fatten on the unfortunate.

To sum up: Los Angeles has physicians and surgeons galore,—good as well as bad; but on the whole, and taking many things into consideration which should be considered, the fraternity is a credit to the city and to this section of the United States.

GREAT POSSIBILITIES.

Griffith J. Griffith, a retired capitalist, says:
"There can be no doubt that Los Angeles, with her many advantages of location and connection with the outside world, together with an inevitable improvement and enlargement of the latter factor in the near futute, offers opportunity for, and invites a wide diversity of manu-

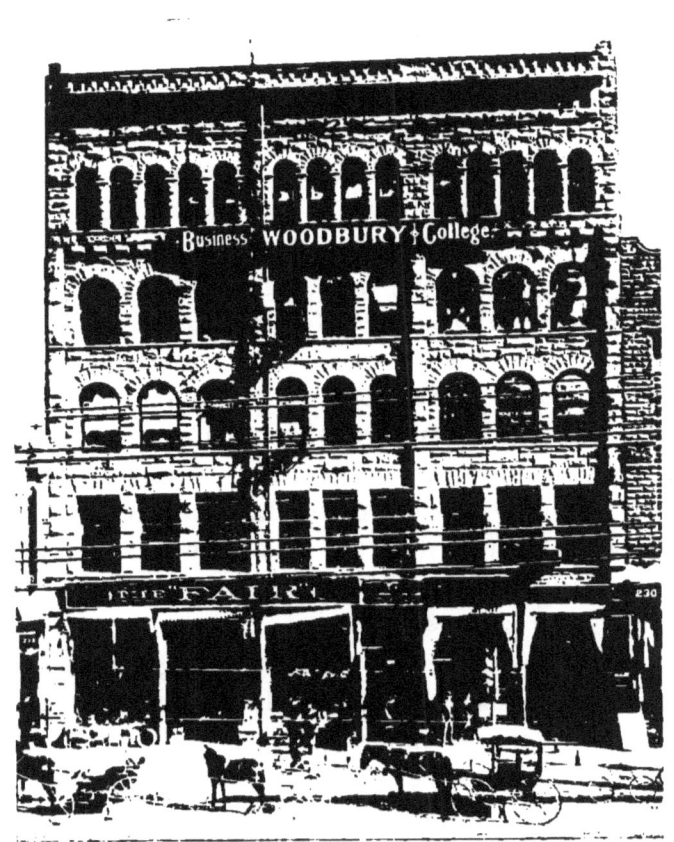

STOWELL BLOCK

factures, and controls an extensive field for the marketing of their products.

Trade is not created, but rather is evolved by the expansion of consuming ramifications, othwise, the enlargment of purchasing territory, therefore manufactures, in a comparatively new country like the southwest, cannot be launched into exis'ence on a large scale at once, but instead must have small beginnings and grow with the development and extension of the marketing area. Under such conditions there are certain indispensible factors necessary for the success of a manufacturing center, foremost of them being accessibility to raw materials, convenient and cheap means of transportation, plentiful supply of fuel at small cost, and the possibility of develoving an extensive consuming market. These atributes are possessed by Los Angeles to a remarkable degree, with an infallible assurance of great improvement and rapid growth in all within a short time.

Her location in the center of the greatest horticultural section of the world, a section which also produces abundantly all cereals and farm products, places her in a position now for the economical and profitable manufacture of all articles of commerce having such products for a base, while the completion of a road to Utah, which cannot be much longer delayed, will bring her into easy connection with the great iron fields of that state, thereby permitting her to engage advantageously in the manufacture of the

Permission of SOUTH PASADENA OSTRICH FARM

great number of articles having that staple for a base, and also making her the best point for the location of works for reducing the precious metals. The petroleum fields of Southern California, which must now be conceded to be practically inexhaustible, have solved the question of cheap fuel, and the opening of the Utah coal fields will improve even the present excellent conditions of affairs in this particular, by placing the very best coal in our market at small cost, for employment in lines where the use of oil is impracticable. In the matter of transportation she is already the best equipped city on the coast, having two transcontinental lines and being connected by rail with three shipping points on the Pacific, all within twenty-five miles of her business center. The construction of a road to Salt Lake City, already referred to will soon add a third transcontinental line and the new harbor at San Pedro, which will probably be in use by the end of the century, will give to this city as good a harbor as any on the Pacific Coast. This will naturally bring into existence lines of water transportation connecting with the Latin republics on the south and with trans-Pacific ports, and taken with the great territory on the east which the railroads will make tributary to this city, will gradually develop a great field for commercial activity.

"The present magnitude of our manufacturing industry is not appreciated by the casual observer for the reason that most of the enterprises

LOS ANGELES THEATRE

are still on a small scale, comparatively, and the last few years of business depression have caused a contraction of operations which have obscured, to some degree, our present resources, but the widening of the field of consumption will soon infuse new life into all of these and the showing that we can make then, with what we have now, will be decidedly noticable. There are many lines as yet untouched here and while it is unnecessary to enumerate any great number of them, mention of a few of the more important may not be amiss.

"One leading commodity for which Los Angeles is well equipped for producing, is glass. The very best sand for this purpose is obtainable in unlimited quantities and sulphur is to be had at very low prices. These, with our cheap fuel and unsurpassed transportation facilities, should give us a glass factory very soon. Iron manufactures of all kinds, from the least to the greatest, should be produced here, and our extensive sheep ranges should enable us to engage profitably in the manufacture of woolen fabrics of all sorts and grades. Fully as important as any of these will be the extensive line of prepared edibles which our abundance of raw materials will enable us to produce, and when the expansion of our market has developed consumption sufficient to call these and many others not named into active operation Los Angeles will indeed be what she should—a large manufacturing center.

" Another element which adds greatly in an

A. W. BAILEY

indirect way to our advantages for manufacturing, is our unparalleled climate and this should not be overlooked, for here the artisans in all lines, being freed from the necessity of providing houses, clothing and food capable of withstanding the rigors of severe winters are enabled to devote that proportion of their earnings which are required in the east for such purposes, to the acquirement of a home and other property interests and the better education of their families, thereby adding materially to the wealth, intelligence and prosperity of the whole community."

On account of health and rush of business we were unable to get an interview with the President of the Chamber of Commerce on manufacturing, but we doubt not but what he would endorse the following, clipped from one of their pamphlets:

"The openings for manufacturing purposes in Los Angeles are many and varied. Not only do local manufacturers enjoy the advantage of cheap fuel, but they are also protected by the high rates of transportation on manufactured goods from the East. Then, again, the mild climate of this section facilitates manufacturing enterprises, rendering solid and expensive buildings unnecessary.

"Among the openings for manufacturing in Los Angeles are fruit and vegetable drying and canning establishments and preserving works, jelly and jam factories, a mustard mill to work up the local product, a castor oil mill, a factory

DR. A. C. MOORE

to manufacture perfumes from flowers, a first-class oil refinery, a tannery, to work up the large quantities of raw hides that are now shipped East, and a shoe factory. One of the most needed manufacturing enterprises in Los Angeles is a glass factory. At present all the glass is imported from the East, although there are deposits of good glass sand in this neighborhood. The fruit industry alone could utilize the entire output of a factory, if the manufactured articles could be obtained at a moderate price. There is an excellent opening here for mineral reduction works. A smelter was commenced several years ago in this city, but it was never completed. There has been a great development of the mineral fields of Southern California during the past year. At present the nearest smelters are at San Francisco, Kansas City and Denver. Petroleum has been successfully used in the smelting of ore.

"A complete tannery should be a success from the start. Large quantities of raw hides are at present shipped East and re-imported as shoes, saddles and harness. We should prepare here calf skins; also sole and harness leather. A harness and saddle factory and a shoe factory would soon follow such a tannery. At present these articles are made only on a very limited scale.

"One of the promising openings for manufacturing enterprises in Los Angeles is the refining of crude petroleum, which is now only

Permission of SOUTH PASADENA OSTRICH FARM

done on a limited scale, in a small factory."

Mr. Abraham Jacoby, ex-President of the Los Angeles Board of Trade and a Director of the Chamber of Commerce, expressed himself as follows:

"Los Angeles, the second city in the State of California, has many natural advantages for establishing manufactories, and promoting industrial enterprises, chief among which are fuel, its situation as a railroad center, its climate, and its transportation facilities other than railroads, through near by sea ports. The greatest factor is undoubtedly fuel, although transportation is as important, and in these two points Los Angeles is well supplied. The residents of Los Angeles are a permanent population, the floating throng now constituting a small item by the side of its permanent population of over one hundred thousand, who are now standing up to give preference to home industries and products. The time is now at hand when our raw material, such as wool, hides, etc., can be utilized right here, and there is a splendid opening for woolen mills, manufactories connected with the making of articles from woolen goods, and tanneries, as well as shoe factories and factories for the manufacture of leather and harness sundries. Numerous enterprises of this nature would give a stimulation to trade and draw to us from other sections of the country a desirable class of citizens, who would come to stay with us, to the extent of many thousand. It would increase our population to such an extent

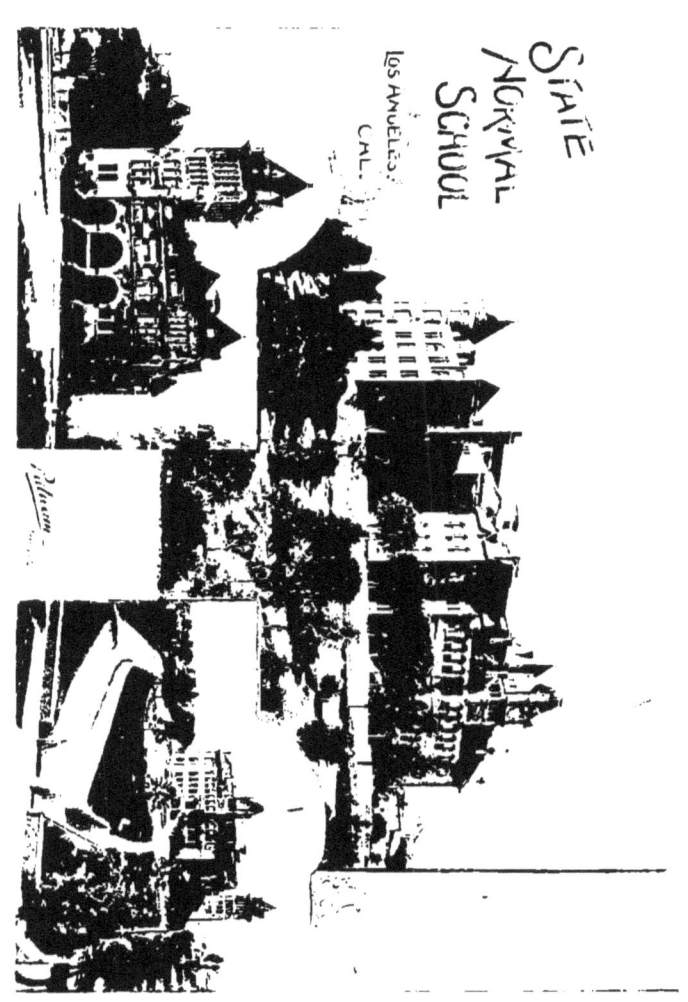

and give our city such an impetus that it would soon become a great commercial center, with a host of valuable and flourishing industries. With the raw material at our doors, and the possibilities before us, we should bend every effort to bring them to a successful combination." The above from Mr. J――is as full of good hard sense as the proverbial nut is full of meat.

Permission of Mount Lowe Railway

YE ALPINE TAVERN

THE CITY FIRE DEPARTMENT

CHIEF WALTER S. MOORE has been connected with the fire department of this city since the year 1875, being at that time an active member of Confidence Engine Co. No 2. He afterwards held the office of Secretary for two terms, and subsequently filled the Presidency for five consecutive years.

In 1883, he was elected Chief Engineer of the Volunteer Fire Department. At the time the paid department came into existence in 1886, Mr. Moore, as Secretary of the first Board of Fire Commissioners, and Chief Engineer of the department, arranged and carried into successful operation the work of the new department.

In 1887, he resigned the Chiefship, to which he was again elected in 1881, resigning Feb. 1, 1893. He is now filling that office for the third time, being re-elected on Feb. 1, 1895, and re-elected 1897. Besides his position as Fire Chief, he is at present President of the Pacific Coast Association of Fire Chiefs, and one of the Vice-Presidents of the International Association of Fire Engineers.

VOLUNTEER FIRE LADDIES.

The fire extinguishing in the early fifties and

MR. W. C. PATTERSON

sixties was done by the Volunteer Fire Brigade ably assisted by the "peons," and numerous water buckets. It was not until September, 1871, that any organization was effected. At that time Los Angeles Engine Co. No. 1 was organized by Geo. M. Fall, then County Clerk, and who was elected Foreman. The membership consisted of all the prominent storekeepers and property owners in the town. The apparatus consisted of an Amoskeag engine (now used by Engine Co. No. 1 in East Los Angeles) and a hose "jumper," (now used in the street department for carrying hose to flush sewers.) The apparatus was drawn by hand until the spring of '74 when the company became dissatisfied and asked the City Council to purchase horses for the engine, and on their refusal the company disbanded.

In April, 1874, many of the old members of No. 1, with the addition of others to the number of thirty-eight, reorganized the company under the name of "Thirty eights," No. 1, with the following officers: Foreman, Chas. E. Miles; First Assistant, John Cashin; Secretary, Sidney Lacy; Treasurer, J. Kuhrts.

Foreman Miles was succeeded by J. Kuhrts; W. F. McDonald, Sam Fay, Henry Decker and Henry Schuner in the order named.

In May, 1875, Engine Co. No. 2 was organized under the name of "Confidence Engine Co." with Geo. Furman, Foreman; Geo. E. Gard, First Assistant; Joe Manning, Second Assistant; John R. Brily, President, and Brice McLillan, Secretary.

G. J GRIFFITH

In '76 Gard succeeded Forman as Foreman, and Walter S. Moore was elected Secretary, vice B. McLillan deceased. The following Foremen were elected and served in the order named: Joe Manning, Robert Eckert for several terms, Wm. E. Stormer and Dan Moriarty. Walter S. Moore was elected President of the company in '77, and occupied that office until 1884, when he was elected Chief Engineer of the Volunteer Department.

The first hook and ladder was built in 1875 by Roeder & Lichtenberg, a local concern, and was housed with the Thirty-eights on Spring, near Franklin street, where the People's store stands. It was cumbersome, heavy and ill adapted to the wants of the city, and was afterwards sold to the town of Wilmington.

In 1876, the city purchased from a San Francisco firm a "village hook and ladder truck" which served the purpose until 1871, when the present 65 feet and extension ladder truck was purchased from the patentee, D. D. Hayes of San Francisco. This truck has recently been remodeled and rebuilt and is located on North Main street near the Plaza. The "truck" originally was housed on Los Angeles, near Aliso street, and subsequently moved to Aliso street, below Alameda. This company was known as Vigilance H. & L. Co. No. 1.

In '81 the residents in the vicinity of the Sixth Street Park organized a hose company under the name of Park Hose Co. No. 1. It was

LOS ANGELES: THEN AND NOW 91

BRADBURY BLOCK

furnished with the 4 wheel hose carriage of Engine Co. No 2, drawn by a pair of horses and located on South Spring street, below Fifth street.

In the spring of '83 the people of East Los Angeles organized a hose company—was supplied with a "jumper" drawn by hand and located on Truman street, near Downey avenue. This company was called East Los Angeles Hose Co. No. 2.

In the fall of '83 the last but not the least of the volunteers was organized in the Morris Vineyard, that property lying between Pico and Washington streets, and Main and Flower streets. A house was built and hose cart provided for the company, which was christened Morris Vineyard Hose Co. No. 3.

In 1882, the S. P. R. R. employees in the vicinity of the River Station—then the San Fernando Street Depot, organized a very efficient hose company, known as the Southern Pacific No. 1. Although not a member of the department, it worked in harmony and did much valuable service in the vicinity of the depot.

All of these companies remained in service until February 1, 1886, when the present paid fire department went into existence.

The Volunteer Fire Department was organized June 20, 1876, by the selection of the following officers:

Charles E. Miles, Chief Engineer; George E. Gard, Assistant Chief. All selections in the Volunteer Department were by elections—the mem

LANKERSHIM BUILDING

bers in good standing in the respective companies voting by ballot for their choice, the ones receiving the highest number of votes being declared elected by the Board of Delegates and served for one year. These elections were very spirited and often much bitter feeling was evidenced. They were succeeded by J. Kuhrts as Chief Engineer, and Fred Kohler of No. 2 as Assistant Chief in March, 1880. These officers served until April, 1883, when Walter S. Moore was elected Chief Engineer, and re-elected in 1784, who was succeeded by Frank R. Day, who served as Assistant Chief under Chief Moore.

Mr. Day resigned his position in October, '85, and the department was demoralized and without executive head until February 1, 1886, when the paid department came into existence.

For much of the foregoing date we are indebted to Fire Commissioner J. Kuhrts.

EXEMPT FIREMEN'S ASSOCIATION.

A charitable and benevolent organization was formed in 1881, and composed of members of the volunteer companies who served actively for five or more consecutive years, and is now in existence with the following officers: President, J. Kuhrts; Secretary, Walter S. Moore; Treasurer, Geo. P. McLain.

PAID FIRE DEPARTMENT.

The paid fire department was created by the City Council in January, 1886, by the selection of a Board of Fire Commissioners, consisting of Mayor

MR. W. O. DOW

E. F. Spence, President of the Council; H. Sinsabaugh and J. Kuhrts, members of the Council, and the ex-Chief of the Volunteer Department, and President of the Exempt Firemen's Association.

The Board organized by electing Mr. Spence as Chairman, and Walter S. Moore, Secretary. After the preliminaries were arranged, the Board elected Mr. Moore, Chief Engineer of the department, and D. A. Moriarty, Assistant Chief, and to them is the honor of successfully organizing the present excellent department. The volunteer organization at that time consisted of 380 members, and the following apparatus: Engine No. 1, situated at the Plaza; Confidence Engine No. 2; at Second and Main streets; Vigilance Hook and Ladder Company No. 2, Aliso street, below Alameda; and the Park Hose Company No. 1, Fifth and Spring streets.

In 1887 the Board consisted of Mayor W. H. Workman, L. N. Breed, President of the Council, and J. Kuhrts. In October of that year Chief Moore resigned, and the Council elected Thomas Strohm, who held the office of Chief for the subsequent three months. The new Council, recognizing the ability and services of D. A. Moriarty, the Assistant Engineer, since its birth, elected him Chief Engineer, to succeed Thomas Strohm, and Chas. E. Miles, Assistant Chief, and the following Commissioners: Mayor Workman, Chairman; John M. Humphries of the Council, and M. Teed, Esq., who held office until succeeded in

MAYOR SNYDER
Permission of "Greater Los Angeles."

December, 1888, by Mayor John Bryson, Chairman, J. Kuhrts, President of the Council, and James Hanly, member of the Council.

In March, 1889, the Council elected, under the new charter, the following citizens Fire Commissioners: J. Kuhrts, Frank Marsh, Tom Keefe and John Lovell, who, with Mayor Hazard elected ex-Chief Thomas Strohm Chief Engineer and Chas. E. Miles, Assistant Chief.

In December, 1889, Walter S. Moore was elected by the Council to succeed D. E. Miles, who succeeded Frank Marsh, resigned. In 1890, Chas. E. Miles resigned as Assistant Chief, and Henry Decker was elected as his successor.

The Council of 1891 elected a Board of Fire Commissioners, consisting of Messrs. W. J. Brodrick, E. L. Stern, C. A. Stilson and J. Kuhrts, Mayor Hazard, ex officio Chairman, and W. W. Robinson, Clerk. The Board selected ex-Chief Walter S. Moore as Chief Engineer, and ex-Chief D. A. Moriarty as Assistant Engineer. The department in February, 1886, consisted of two steam fire engines, one hook and ladder truck, and one hose carriage drawn by horses. In March, 1889, two additional fire engines were purchased and put into service; one at Ninth street and the other at Sixteenth street, thus doubling the number of the engines.

After the disastrous fire of the Los Angeles Furniture Company, in January, 1889, ex-Chief Moore was selected by the city authorities and the Pacific Coast Board of Underwriters, to exam-

CAPT. J. B. LANKERSHIM

ine into the fire department, and report such improvements and additions thereto, as would put it into a first-class condition. The report was adopted, and the much needed improvements made, by the purchase of three steam fire engines, and three hose carts. They were put into service, one each in Boyle Heights, East Los Angeles and the western hills on Temple street.

In 1892 the efficiency of service was further increased by the addition of steam heaters, and releasing apparatus to the fire engines, the attachment of the water tower to the ladder truck, and the purchase of two Champion chemical engines, drawn by horses, and many other minor improvements. All apparatus is drawn by horses, with swinging harness, and all firemen are fully uniformed while on duty.

In 1895 three Champion combination chemical engines and hose wagons were purchased and companies organized to handle the apparatus, consisting of full paid crews of three men and located as follows:

Chemical Co. No. 3 in East Los Angeles on Griffen avenue, below Downey avenue. Chemical Co. No. 4, on West Pico street, near Star street. Chemical Co. No. 5, on South Central avenue, below Twelfth street.

In the later part of 1896, Engine Co. No. 3 was consolidated with Park Hose Co. No. 1, and the apparatus was located in the elegant new quarters erected by E. Ruthmiller on Hill street, near Fourth street. This house is probably the

W. S. MOORE

most thoroughly equipped house on the Pacific Coast, and the equal to any in the largest departments in the United States, and is manned by a permanent crew of 16 men.

In the early part of 1897, a first-class Babcock aerial ladder and truck was purchased in Chicago and placed with the above company. The ladder has a height of 85 feet from the ground to its top and is the most complete piece of aerial apparatus built.

In October, 1897, Chemical Co. No. 1, located at the Plaza, was consolidated with Hook and Ladder Co. No 1, and Truck "A," and the company is known as "J. Kuhrts" Engine Co. No. No. 3, the old engine house being remodeled and modernized, and the company provided with all necessary appliances and a permanent crew of 15 men.

The Los Angeles Fire Department is up to date and will compare favorably with any department in cities of its size throughout the world, and is so recognized by the National Board of Underwriters.

Walter S. Moore, Chief Engineer of the Los Angeles Fire Department, was born of old Revolutionary stock, in the District of Kensington, city of Philadelphia, in 1851, and was educated in the public schools of that city. During the latter part of the civil war, he was an attendant of the Northwest Grammar School, and afterwards a runner with Philadelphia Fire Co. No. 10.

The present efficient Board of Fire Commis-

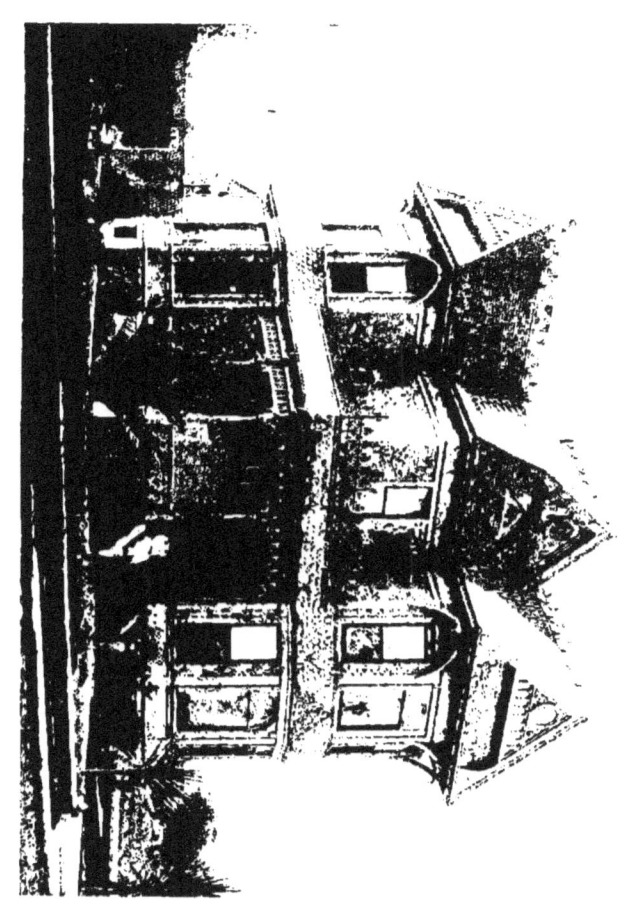

RESIDENCE OF A. M. OZMUN

sioners consists of Mayor M. P. Snyder, ex-Officio Chairman; Hon. J. Kuhrts, Hon. C. M. Wells, Hon. Geo. Sinsabaugh, Hon. Frank Sabichi, Robt. A. Todd, Secretary.

For much of the foregoing statistics we are indebted to the courtesy of the efficient and intelligent Chief Engineer of the Fire Department, Walter S. Moore.

Y. M. C. A.

BY WILLARD D. BALL.

The building of the Y. M. C. A. is a familiar sight to passers on Broadway, who often stop to admire its ornamental front. Comparatively few even, of those who speak with pride of the Young Men's Christian Association know the great variety of its activities as carried on within its walls, nor realize that it is but little over fifty years since the first association under that name was organized in London. Its founder was Sir George Williams, then an obscure dry goods clerk and fifty years later as head of the same firm, knighted for his services to mankind in founding this organization. The Los Angeles Association was organized in 1882, and is one of 6,500 similar institutions scattered throughout the world. During the fifteen years of its existence, it has shared in the vicissitudes of the city, but with a gradual broadening out in the lines of its work and a strengthening of its hold upon the community.

Educational, physical, social and religious departments are maintained. The evening educa-

BULDARD BLOCK
Permission of the "Hub"

tional classes number over three hundred pupils each year in nearly thirty different subjects, consisting of business branches, languages, music and industrial studies. The students are young men who, for the most part, are busy during the day at their various vocations and utilize their spare moments for something better than mere amusements.

Another line of work is scientific "body building," carried on in a well equipped gymnasium. Here a competent physical director examines, takes measurements and prescribes exercise for any who desire either to win health or retain it. The baths are a valuable adjunct to this department. Pleasant social and game rooms on the third floor never lack for occupants.

The building has a beautiful auditorium, seating about six hundred, in which are held concerts and lectures on each Sunday afternoon, a gospel meeting for young men. An important department of the work is conducted by the employment secretary who devotes his time to looking up places for young men and placing young men who can bring first-class references. From twenty-five to thirty-five young men have been placed in either temporary or permanent positions each month for the last few months.

The privileges of the association are open to all young men of good character irrespective of religious belief and upon payment of dues which are but nominal in comparison with the opportunities offered.

BICKNELL BLOCK

WHAT THIS CITY AND COUNTRY NEEDS

BY MR. W. C. PATTERSON.

"The primary need of Los Angeles city is, I should say, more manufactories, which would give employment and afford means of sustenance to large numbers of the poorer classes of people. I am aware that many of the conditions are not the most favorable as yet to heavy manufacturing, but with the early advent of the Salt Lake Railway which will give us cheap coal and iron, Los Angeles should become a great manufacturing city.

"Southern California in general, needs more people of the right kind. It needs people with money, with energy, with enterprise and with industry. There are opportunities for the safe and reasonably profitable investment of capital. These opportunities will not always come to him who sits down with folded arms 'waiting for something to turn up.'

"The new settler, whether capitalist or not, should be active and alert. The soil is here, the climate is here, the conditions are here, waiting and ready to be utilized.

"We need, too, a class of citizens who are industrious and thrifty, and who are willing to put their own hands to the plow. The increase of production and competition, no longer permit

GENERAL C. F. A. LAST

such profits that the producer can hire all the work done upon his ranch or orchard, and still expect to make a living and a fortune from ten acres of land. There are as fair returns awaiting the industrious farmer here as anywhere, but gradual crystalization is bringing usual conditions down to the close margins which prevail east of the Rockies.

"One thing which is vitally needed, both for the reputation of this section as well as profit to our producers, is more care and skill in the handling of farms and orchards and their products. There is great truth in the old aphorism 'crowded below, but plenty of room above.' He who takes the best care of his property, who most carefully cultivates and fertilizes his lands, using his brains as well as his hands, is almost uniformly successful.

"Next in importance to the growing of crops is the harvesting of the same. The man whose oranges, for example, are carefully picked, cleaned, graded and packed, every imperfect one being rejected, always has a market. The attempt to sell and ship inferior stuff is ruining the reputation of the country. It had better be thrown into the sea. It would be money made in the end. The same is true of other things beside oranges. If this country is to maintain pre-eminence it must be achieved and sustained with quality rather than quantity.

"Potatoes, with a few big ones in one end of the sack and the remaining composed of misera-

NORTH SIDE OF ECHO MOUNTAIN
Permission of Mount Lowe Railway

ble scabby stuff, do not make for the producer or his section an enviable reputation.

"Walnuts, with soil which attached to them when they fell under the trees still clinging to them, are unsalable, whereas, those which are thoroughly cleaned and carefully graded are usually of ready sale. They do not need 'sulphuring,' that vile subterfuge, which is intended to make nuts seem what they are not, and which is unnecessary if they are properly cleaned and cared for.

"Our dried fruits for example, can no longer find ready sale unless neatness and cleanliness obtain from the time the fruit is taken from the tree until it is sold, and unless it is honestly graded and tastily packed, and so on to the end of the chapter.

"Of course, common sense must be used in marketing our stuff. It will not do to 'kill the goose that laid the golden egg,' by demanding at the beginning of the season, more for our products than the same class of goods are jobbing for in the great markets upon which we must depend. A notable example may be cited in the fact that this year the walnut growers' associations, instead of allowing common sense to prevail, demanded prices twenty per cent. higher than similar grades were bringing in the Atlantic markets, with the result that those markets were speedily filled to overflowing with importations to the exclusion of the California article. A more sensible policy would have secured to the

Permission of HAWLEY, KING & CO.

walnut growers of Southern California at least one hundred thousand dollars more than they will receive through the 'hog the persimmon,' plan which was adopted. The orange growers committed the same blunder in 1895.

"Without going into detail, this country now needs more people of the right kind, and also that which our own people can supply, viz: careful cultivation of the soil, and honest harvesting of its products.

" Let nothing be placed on the market until it is the very best exponent of labor, brains and skill, and a reputation will result which will be world wide; buyers from the antipodes will seek us out and contend for the opportunity to buy what we have to sell and at prices which will give us 'money to burn.' In short, let us have a little more honesty; first, honesty with ourselves, not obscured by laziness, and second, honesty with all the rest of mankind."

We especially commend the remarks by Mr. Patterson. To follow out his suggestions would be to push our commercial, manufacturing and agricultural resources rapidly forward.

CITY ON THE MOUNT, ECHO MOUNTAIN
Permission of Mount Lowe Railway

CITY SEWER SYSTEM

BY J. H. DOCKWEILER, CITY ENGINEER.

THE sewer system of the city of Los Angeles consists of two main portions, the internal (the "collecting" system) and the outfall sewer (the "disposing" system.) Both portions are the creation of the last fifteen years of the history of the city—the latter absolutely so, and the former to all practical intent and purpose, as will appear from the following figures. At the present moment (1st December, 1897), the total length of the internal system is 141 3-10 miles, while at the beginning of the period mentioned there were in existence only about 10 miles (exact 9.93), which are classified as clay or cement pipes.

The classification of the present total of 141.3 miles above mentioned is as follows:

Clay or cement pipe sewer	9.93 miles
Brick sewer (30 inches to 52 inches internal diameter)	8.08 "
Cast iron sewer (30-inch pipe under Los Angeles river)	0.08 "
Vitrified pipe sewer (from 8 to 30 in. internal drain)	123.21 "
Total	141.30 "

To any one casually inspecting this statement

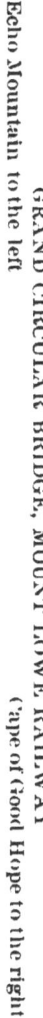

GRAND CIRCULAR BRIDGE, MOUNT LOWE RAILWAY
Echo Mountain to the left   Cape of Good Hope to the right

without knowing the peculiar circumstances of this city with regard to climate, respecting rainfall, it might appear that the smaller size sewers unduly predominated and that hence the whole system would be liable to be inefficient for the population which is at present served by it and would become more inefficient as the population increases.

Such a conclusion would be an error. The sewers of this city were planned—and very wisely so—on what is known as the "separate system;" that is, they are proportioned to convey the sewage only and not the rainfall. The latter finds its way into the natural water courses by the gutters of the streets and—as parts of the city become more and more densely built up—by subterranean storm drains, which do not convey sewage and, hence, are no part of the sewer system.

As a matter of experience, hardly any of the sewers, planned and built within the last ten or twelve years, are taxed by the sewage of the present population to much above one quarter of their capacity. The sewage of the present population is distinctly less than anticipated and the vitrified pipe sewers, as a whole, were well built and are in such good, smooth, internal condition, that they err—if error there be—in being too large rather than too small.

After the internal system of sewers has collected the sewage, the further question is: how is this combined mass to be disposed of? This has for years been the problem before the city author-

HOTEL VAN NUYS

ities and several partial solutions were from time to time adopted—none of them satisfactory in the long run. The outfall sewer, built in the years 1893 and 1894, has proved itself—in conformity with the views of its designers—as the final solution, making the city the absolute master of the situation at all times. It is of ample capacity to take the sewage of a population of 125,000 or more, and carry it out into the ocean, if—and as long as—this sewage cannot be put to any better use. But during what is called the irrigation season it can be—and is—put to a better use. For about six months in the year very little, if any, sewage is wasted. It is all sold for irrigation along a portion of its route to the ocean. At present—irrigation generally, and irrigation by sewage particularly, being something new in part of the country between the city and the ocean, traversed by the sewer—the methods practiced are rather crude and improvident. But in the course of time all this is certain to change to something better and more permanent. Then the sewage will be used for irrigation at all times and not merely—as is too often done at present—to save a crop in the nick of time, which was expected to mature without an expenditure for irrigation. When this shall have been attained, the sewage problem will be disposed of without the doubtful experiment of a sewage farm, owned and managed by the municipal corporation.

This outfall sewer is nearly 12 miles long, for over half of which distance it is a wood-stave

HON. JOSEPH D. LYNCH
Permission of "Greater Los Angeles."

pressure pipe (inverted syphon) carrying the sewage across two very shallow valleys, each over three miles wide, where it can be pressed to the surface and used for irrigation without any expenditure for pumping. In the upper valley the pipe is of 38 inches internal diameter; in the lower valley of 36 inches. The rest of the above length of nearly 12 miles consists of brick sewer of 40 inches internal diameter and of tunnels of brick and concrete, of oval cross section, $4\frac{1}{2}$ feet wide and six feet high. Of these tunnels there are three, the longest over a mile in length. From the bluff overlooking the ocean to high-water mark, and thence 600 feet into the ocean, there are 1200 feet of cast iron pipe of 24 inches internal diameter.

The total cost of the sewer system, i. e. construction, cost, to date is about $1,250,000.

PROFESSOR PIERCE

OUR MINING INTEREST

BY WILBUR O. DOW.

SOUTHERN California fruits have acquired a reputation throughout the entire civilized world, and have drawn the attention of the people almost entirely away from the mining industry. Outside of those most directly interested, there are but few who are aware of the rich storehouse of precious metals that lie hidden in our mountain ranges, and among the sands of the desert, awaiting the pick of the sturdy miner to bring them to light, and prove to the world that the country south of the Tehachepi range contains as much rich mineral as does any other section of equal area in the world. Not but what there are other sections of the country equally as rich, but the territory is much smaller, and the cost of separating the ore so much greater, that their value must sink into insignificance, when compared with this vast territory.

For years past, the newspapers throughout the State have kept the public fully informed as to the immense amount of fruit raised, consumed at home and shipped to Eastern States and foreign countries, but invariably they have been more or less reticent regarding the output of our

H. C. WYATT

producing mines, and the amount of development work being done in newly discovered territory, until within, perhaps, the past year.

While it is true that the many millions and millions of dollars worth of wheat and fruit, which are exported to foreign countries are something we may well be proud of, yet we should also be proud of the fact that California's gold production also runs into millions, and we should not be forced to wait for the little paragraph sent out by the director of the mint, once a year, to gain this information.

Since the first discovery of gold in California, the State has ranked as the greatest gold producing region ever known, and leaving out the period prior to 1870 altogether, we find from 1870 down to and including 1896, the State has produced the fabulous sum of $393,450,951 in gold, or an average of $14,842,665 per year. The yield last year was $15,335,900, and for the present year the probabilities are that the amount will be largely in excess of that produced in 1896.

That the agricultural and horticultural interests in Southern California have largely outgrown the mining industry, is not to be wondered at, as our semi-tropical climate, splendid soil and other natural advantages, drew to this section thousands of people who were unacquainted with mining, but who were thorough agriculturalists and horticulturalists. They were enthusiastic in their belief that the desert could be made to blos-

HART BROS.

som as the rose, and how well they have succeeded can only be known by a trip over any of the lines of railway traversing the great citrus belt. But the lover of horticulture, by his magnificent success, has paved the way for another and just as important member of the genus homo, the man who delves in the bowels of the earth to gain riches, and during the past few years this industry has received an impetus that will eventually land this favored section at the head of its class.

The discovery of gold, made by Marshall on Sutter Creek, in the Northern part of the State, was proclaimed throughout the world and caused a stampede, the like of which has never been equaled to any gold producing country.

Before and during the war, mining was the favorite pursuit of the venturesome "tenderfoot." The newcomer, with few exceptions, tried the mines as a starter—as a rule, they were all young, and in no ways overburdened with wealth, and as mining was about the only available means of "making a pile," and as there were few if any other occupations open, promising in so short a time the large returns of the fortunate miner, most of them "headed" for the mining districts. Occasionally the man reared under the care of doting parents, and the advantages of wealth in his distant home, and trained to the vocation and profession of doctor, preacher or lawyer, finding the life of miner a trifle too irksome, would gravitate to the "Pueblitas" or small

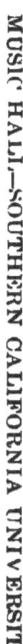

MUSIC HALL—SOUTHERN CALIFORNIA UNIVERSITY

towns, and turn gambler, or marry a Spanish senorita and a "rancho" and settle down to stock raising.

After the "conquest" of California, the country was divided into military districts. The government, with the view of more fully protecting the newcomers, (who went anywhere without regard to consequences) established "Military Posts" upon the frontier in all directions. If the venturesome miner got into trouble of any kind, he could apply to the Post Quartermaster for aid, and be sure of receiving assistance. If sick, he would be treated in the Post Hospital. If out of provisions, he would be furnished, and after resting, he was at liberty to resume his journey.

In those early days, the officers and men of the army were a generous class, and can be said to have been the best friends the miner had, and to have given the mining industry the only impetus it had aside from its promising results— they spent their salaries freely, and in every way helped the unfortunate and often discouraged miners to continue their prospecting and to go on mining in their primitive way. Quite a contrast when compared to the way the Canadian government treated the Klondyke miners the past year. While mining in the Northern portion of the State was more profitable at one time, it has been followed in Southern California constantly, and to a greater or less extent. There were many big mining enterprises, and a great deal of gold has

HON. STEPHEN M. WHITE
Permission of "The Capital"

been sent to the mint from south of the Tehachepi mountains.

As a historical fact, and perhaps not widely known, gold was first discovered in Los Angeles county, and not by Marshall, on Sutter Creek, as claimed. This can be readily verified by many of the early comers now in Southern California. Don Abel Stearns of Los Angeles made a shipment of gold to the U. S. mint at Philadelphia as early as 1842—this gold having been taken from the San Gabriel Cañon and the San Francisquite Creek. Alfred Robinson is, perhaps, the first man to have his gold received at a U. S. mint from these mines, and without question it was here in 1841 or 1842, that the first discovery of gold in California occurred. Francisco Lopez, a native Californian, while digging wild onions with his sheath knife, discovered a piece of gold in the dirt, and it is also a known fact that as early as 1843 and 1844, the Indians exchanged gold for liquor and goods in Monterey. Lopez was unquestionably the first white man of record to discover gold in California. He sleeps in obscurity, while Marshall has a statue erected in his memory.

The first quartz mill built for Southern California came in 1856, and was for mines in the slate range country, now in Inyo county. This mill was owned by the late Prudent Beaudry and Dan and John Searles, and was built by Peter Donahue, who alone in California could do that kind of work at that date. This old time mill

J. H. DOCKWEILER
Permission of "The Capital"

ran a long while, and created great prosperity in its vicinity. The next mill was also built by Mr. Donahue in 1861, and was sent to the Holcomb Valley, it was also a good paying property. It is claimed that millions of dollars were taken from the Placer and Quartz mines in Holcomb Valley between the years of 1860 and 1865. In 1862 there were fully 3000 miners in the district, all making money. About the same time the Holcomb Valley mill was erected, a five-stamp mill was brought into Southern California, and erected at the famous Armargosa mines; this mill also paid enormously until 1863, when the Indians raided the place and burned the mill. At this time—1861 to 1865—mining operations upon a large scale were being carried on at La Pez and along the Colorado River for over 200 miles.

El Dorado Cañon was a lively camp during these years. After the discovery of silver in Nevada, in 1859, by Pat McLaughlin (not by Comstock) mining for that metal, as well as gold, took on quite a boom all over California and Nevada.

Since the first excitement which occurred in 1841-42, this section has experienced no particular mining boom, but what is much more satisfactory, there has been a gradual and substantial growth of the mining industry. To be sure, the growth up to within the past two or three years has been slow, but it has been steady and of a kind to gain the confidence of capitalists, when once they become acquainted with the territory.

There is an old saying that the " proof of the

HOTEL LINCOLN

pudding is in the eating," and it appears peculiarly applicable to existing circumstances in this particular section today; inasmuch as a few short years ago there were no mining districts platted, and but few stamp mills in operation, and very little interest taken in this industry. Today a great change is apparent; the territory is divided into a score or more districts, all of which have many good paying mines, and hundreds of promising prospects. Stamp mills are being erected as fast as the demand for them shows that they may become profitable; this coupled with the fact that ore taken from, even the poorest mines, can be worked at a fair profit, has created an impetus to the mining industry, heretofore unknown.

To those who have not kept themselves informed regarding the mining industry of Southern California, a recapitulation of the mills in operation will no doubt prove somewhat of a surprise. Briefly stated, the mills in operation are as follows:

LOS ANGELES COUNTY.

Mill, 4; stamps, 30.

SAN DIEGO COUNTY.

Mills, 21; stamps, 329.

SAN BERNARDINO COUNTY.

Mills, 29; stamps, 304.

KERN COUNTY.

Mills, 24; stamps, 238.

RIVERSIDE COUNTY.

Mills, 18; stamps, 123.

W. C. T. U.

INYO COUNTY.

Mills, 22; stamps, 132.

VENTURA COUNTY.

Mills, 2; stamps, 20.

And in addition, there are a large number of arastras, dry washers and patent mills of all kinds scattered throughout all the counties, and from a careful estimate it is conceded that during the present year Southern California will furnish $5,800,000 worth of mineral.

LOS ANGELES COUNTY MINES.

Los Angeles county boasts of forty or fifty gold mines being worked at the present time, chief among which are the Red Rover and Mohawk-Acton in the Acton district. Work was begun on the Red Rover mine over thirty years ago, and was followed up with varying success for five years, when the vein pinched out, and for a time the mine was abandoned. Later, however, the owners concluded to sink deeper, and at the depth of 700 feet were rewarded with a twelve foot ledge of valuable ore. The Mohawk-Acton is an old Mexican mine, that was worked about twenty years ago, from which several thousand dollars were extracted by the arastra process. It was abandoned for several years until its present owners gained possession, when they at once began development work in a thorough and systematic manner.

In San Gabriel Cañon a number of miners are making fairly good wages working placer mines.

GREAT CABLE INCLINE, MOUNT LOWE

The San Gabriel Mining Company have driven a tunnel 1300 feet under the bed of the river, with strong hopes that when they strike bed rock they will be amply repaid for their labor. They have expended $20,000 in the work.

Ten miles east of Acton is the Black Cat, upon which a large amount of work has been done, and a twenty stamp mill is connected with the mine.

On Mt. Gleason, eight miles from Acton, there are eight mines, upon some of which considerable development work has been done. Sixteen miles East of Acton are the Monte Cristo group of five mines, two of which are free milling. There are also the Peabody and West mines, eight miles from Acton on Mt. Gleason. The Tejunga mines, sixteen miles East of Acton, upon all of which development work is being steadily carried on.

RIVERSIDE COUNTY.

A large majority of the mining claims in Riverside county have been located during the past eighteen months. Many of them are proving extremely rich, and their owners are very enthusiastic over their chances. The principal districts are the Pinon, Pinicate, Eagle Mountain and Menifee. Assays from the ores in these districts run from $5 to $20 per ton. In the Pinon district is the now celebrated Lost Horse mine, for which an offer of $250,000 has been refused. It is situated twenty-eight miles North of Indio, and

RUSTIC CANYON, SANTA MONICA

has lately been incorporated with a capital stock of $500,000 divided into 5000 shares.

In the Eagle Mountain district there are a number of good mines, assays from which prove them to be very rich. Among them are the Iron Chief, from which several carloads of ore have been shipped, and given returns of from $80 to $115 per ton; the Blackbird, $80 to $124 per ton; the Buzzard, $52 in gold and a good showing in copper; the Occident, $100 per ton; the Mary Ann, $350 per ton from the croppings, and a new discovery, the Essie I., the character of ore and formation being identical with the Lost Horse mine, and assaying from $300 to $426 per ton, free milling ore In the Menifee district the most promising mine is the Leon, situated seven miles southwest of Winchester. The ore averages from $32 to $153 per ton. Other good mines are the Mammoth, Ophir, Perris and the Menifee, the latter being equipped with a steam hoist and a five-stamp mill. Adjoining the Menifee on the West is the Pinicate district, which contains a number of famous mines, of which the best developed are the Good Hope, Golden Chariot, Santa Rosa, Santa Fe and Indian Queen. Of these the Good Hope is the best known, and is considered by experts to be very valuable, $11,000 having been milled in a two weeks' run, and a new ledge has been uncovered which assays $2000 to the ton.

SAN BERNARDINO COUNTY.

During the past two years this county has made rapid strides in the development of its

INTERIOR VIEW OF YE ALPINE TAVERN

mining industry. Old mines have been reopened, new discoveries made, mills built, water developed and prospecting done on a large scale. The Virginia Dale district is at present receiving more attention than any other section. The first locations were made about eight years ago near Dale City, and the prospectors were obliged to haul water from Twenty-nine Palms, fourteen miles distant. Since then, a well one hundred feet deep has been sunk at Dale City, which furnishes an abundance of water for the surrounding mines. F. C. Baird, who owns a number of mines, has erected a twenty stamp mill, which is kept running night and day. The ore taken from the mines in this district runs from $8 to $110 per ton.

The Holcomb Valley district, one of the oldest in Southern California, is exceedingly rich in placer diggings. Over thirty years ago, a large number of miners were working the placers and took out millions of dollars in a few months, but owing to an excess of water too near the surface, the work was abandoned. About four years ago a large portion of the valley was purchased by an English company, who have put in the latest improved machinery, including a steam shovel. They have also heavy pumps to keep out the water, and will go to bed rock. The gravel is known to be very rich, and with the addition of the improved machinery to handle it, large returns are expected. In the Upper Holcomb a stamp mill has been erected by Mr. Arnold of Los Angeles to

GEORGE W. WHITE, D. D.

crush the ore from his two quartz mines. He has run a seventy-five foot drift on one of his claims, which has a three foot ledge of $20 ore, mostly free milling The results obtained have been so satisfactory to Mr. Arnold, that he has decided to enlarge his plant. The celebrated Green Leaf mine is in this district, from which, it is stated, Richard Garvey took several hundred thousand dollars in gold thirty-five years ago. The mine was abandoned for twenty five years. About a year ago, Messrs. Dickey and Simons bonded it, and cleaned out the old tunnel, drifted farther in and struck another rich vein. They have improved machinery, a ten-stamp mill, and it is conceded that if it were possible to take out nearly a million with the aid only of arastras and a cannon ball mill, the new owners will be able to produce many times that amount.

At Horse Springs, several claims have been taken up, and a few good strikes made, but very little of the ore is free milling. Among them are the Little Nell, Victor, Mojave Chief and Gold Bug. Considerable development work has been done in all of them, and the ore taken out will yield a handsome profit. The Gold Bug is a four foot ledge, nine inches of which is high grade. The owner made a shipment of several tons of selected ore, which netted $125 per ton. There is an abundance of timber and water in this district, and a good road from the mines to the railroad.

Another rich district, and one that is at pres-

ECHO MOUNTAIN HOUSE

Permission MOUNT LOWE RAILWAY

ent receiving much attention, is the Hocumac. For years a party of men have been working a placer claim known as the Hydraulic. As to the amount taken out, little is known, as the men who are working it prefer to keep quiet regarding its richness, yet old miners claim that between $50,000 and $100,000 in gold has been secured.

The Agamemnon, a claim recently located, has caused considerable excitement, and by its richness has caused a more thorough prospecting of the district. Assays from the Agamemnon have ranged from $68 to $675 per ton.

ORO GRANDE DISTRICT.

This is an old mining camp, located on the Santa Fe R. R. just over the mountains from San Bernardino. As a rule, the ore is very refractory. There are a few claims in this camp considered. The Carbonate, the Rose and Sidewinder, have been worked for the past six or seven years. The Vanderbilt, owned by Charley Bell, is a promising claim. The ledge is seven feet wide, with a shaft 125 feet deep, and 60 foot drift. The average value of the ore is $12 per ton. Several years ago, a very rich pocket of ore, showing free gold, was uncovered in the shaft, which at the time created quite an excitement in the camp, but as a rule the ore is not of high grade, but has paid something over expenses for mining and shipping.

South of Virginia Dale, on the mountains in Hemet Valley, some prospecting has been done.

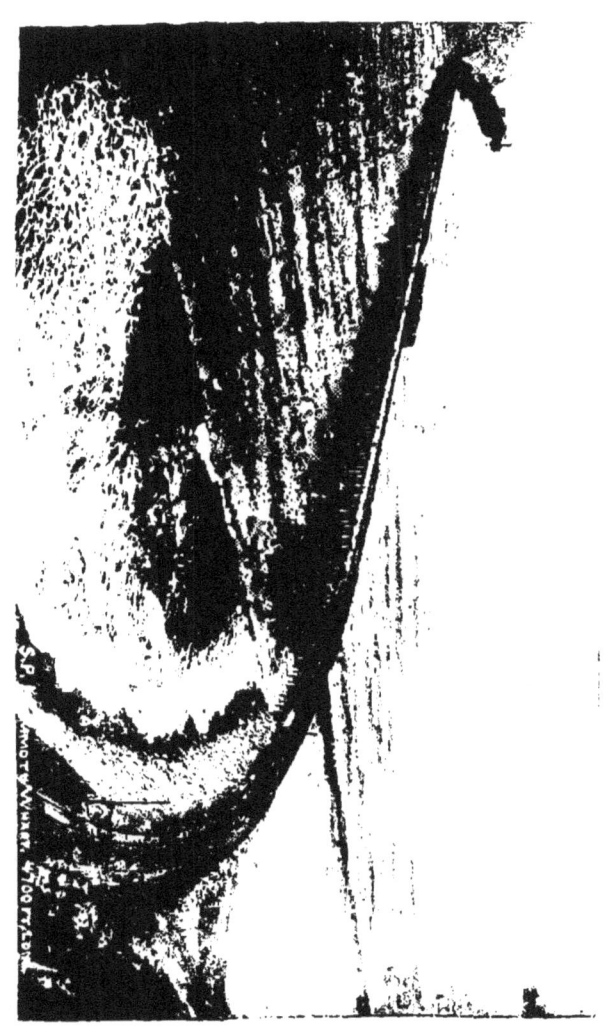

The Hemet Bell is one of the oldest claims in this district. The ledge is only about 16 inches wide and ore is free milling. The value of the ore from this claim is $20 per ton. The formation is granite. South of the Hemet Bell several large ledges have been discovered, but of low grade.

In the Good Hope district a large number of locations have been made, and many of the claims are being worked, but whether this camp will be a success, the future only can determine.

The section of the country south of Glamis, near the Bay Horse mine, is at present attracting much attention. On account of the indications for paying placer ground, during the past sixty days, a large number of placer locations have been made, and the locators are now at work with dry washers, testing the value of their claims If water could be obtained for washing these placers, there is no doubt but what they would pay handsomely, as nearly every pan of dirt shows colors.

THE AMARGOSA MINE.

This mine is situated in the Amargosa district about eighty miles Northeast of Daggett on the line of the Santa Fe R. R. Fickle fortune has played many pranks with this mine. There is abundant evidence that it was worked by the Spaniards long before Americans thought of gold in California.

Later, it was worked by Mexicans, but as their facilities for crushing ore were of the simplest

103. WEST LAKE PARK, FROM THE NORTH.

kind, they worked only the richest ore. A five stamp mill was put up early in the sixties, and the mine was soon in a flourishing condition, but the Indians made a raid, murdered the miners and burned the mill. During the early part of the present year, ths mine was secured by Los Angeles parties, who began active work, and have equipped it with the latest improved machinery. They have done over 2,500 feet of work, and have uncovered ore of great richness. The vein is said to be a true fissure, eight feet wide, much of which is high grade, and some of the samples which have been assayed run as high as $8,000 per ton. The formation is granite, which gives the assurance that it will grow richer as they go down. The company have opened it for 800 feet, and report 20,000 tons of ore in sight. There is abundance of fuel and water, also a good wagon road to Daggett. The company is firmly of the opinion that the Amargosa will soon become dividend paying, and one of the largest producers in the State.

The Vanderbilt, Manvel and Twenty-nine Palms districts have each a number of promising mines and excellent prospects. While a few of the pioneers have known of the richness of these districts for a long time, it required the increased interest in mining of the past few years for them to be thoroughly prospected.

RANDSBURG—THE RAND MINING DISTRICT.

Since the great rush to the California gold fields in '49, there has probably been no district

LOS ANGELES: THEN AND NOW 153

CALLA LILY VIEW—SANTA MONICA

which has caused so much excitement in a short space of time as the Rand Mining district, situated in the southern part of Kern county, and only a day's ride from Los Angeles. The first quartz vein was discovered in 1895, since which time the recorder of that county has been kept pretty busily engaged recording mining claims.

The district has been thoroughly written up by every city daily in the State, and the fame of the wonderful deposits have reached every part of the civilized globe, and it is in part due to the rich discoveries made in this district that the great revival in the mining industry of Southern California may be attributed.

To give a detailed account of the development work already accomplished would take more space than this article is designed to fill, yet a brief synopsis will not be amiss.

The Wedge mine, one of the first to win a record, at a depth of 365 feet, is claimed to have produced $120,000, the first work being done only a little over a year ago.

The Lucky Star Group of Mines, which have been so little developed that they are scarcely more than prospects, produced $50,000 the first year.

The Merced mine has two shafts down 100 feet and from which over $8,000 was taken in a short time.

On the Napoleon two shafts have been sunk from which $7,000 was taken in six weeks. Sixteen tons of ore netted $3,000.

The Gold Bug, Treasure, Butte, Minnehaha, Tip Top, Yorkshire Lass, Hard Cash, Magganetta, J. I. C. and Excelsior, are all being rapidly developed, and are piling up ore, from which a handsome profit will accrue when milled.

JOHANNESBURG.

There is quite a rivalry between Randsburg and Johannesburg for supremacy as mining camps. Johannesburg being the terminus of the branch railroad from Kramer, will, no doubt, claim the distinction of being "the metropolis."

The most talked about mine in this camp is the Alameda, upon which reduction works are being erected at a cost of $20,000. Four shafts are being sunk on the property on parallel veins, which are from 20 to 40 feet apart. The ore bodies are from three to six feet in width and free milling. About 100 tons of ore have been milled, the ore ranging from $9 to $100 per ton. The company is incorporated with a capital of half a million, but there is not a dollar's wor h of stock for sale.

The Val Verde group have proved to be great wealth producers. On Val Verde No 1 a shaft has been sunk 150 feet, with ore in sight estimated to be worth $250,000.

On the King Solomon mine the shaft is down over 200 feet, and upon which a very rich strike was made on the 200 foot level.

The Garlock district, which is on the Mojave road to Ransburg, has rich placer diggings, but owing to the scarcity of water, cannot be worked to the best advantage. The gold is of a very fine quality, running in value as high as $19 per ounce.

SAN DIEGO COUNTY.

Mining affairs through San Diego county are keeping in touch with the districts in other counties. The Eastern part of the county is a vast mining district, of which little is known, with the exception of the Cargo Muchacho district, in which are situated some large properties, among them the Golden Cross mines and others.

The Golden Cross mines are equipped with the largest mill in Southern California—140 stamps. They are in the hands of a receiver at the present time, on account of a disagreement among the stockholders, yet with the additional expense, the mines are paying all expenses and giving a fair profit, and this too, on low grade ore, avering from $2.13 to $5.64 per ton. It is interesting to note the fact that ore averaging only $3.98 per ton can be worked at a profit. Such being the case, however, it is still more interesting to figure the profits which would accrue from ore ranging from $25 to $100. It seems to be simply a case of the capacity of the stamp mills.

Twenty-five miles north of Yuma, and five miles west of the Colorado river, is the Picacho district, from which it is stated $10,000,000 of gold has come from placer diggings. Four miles west of the Picacho basin is the White Gold Basin, upon which some excellent mines have been located. Tests made of the ore returned $74 per ton in free gold. The owner of the group is a Denver man, and it is reported he will erect a 100 stamp mill.

The Julian, Escondido and Deer Park districts are each receiving their share of attention by mining men, and give promise of furnishing some good mines in the near future.

The Mesquite, well known to all old time prospectors, is receiving more than usual attention since the discovery of the Bay Horse mine. This mine was located the first of last year. Several tests of ore have been made, five of them averaging $127.31. A company has been formed with the capital placed at $1,500,000. Active development work is now in progress, three shafts having been sunk, 40, 35 and 30 feet deep, all in good ore. The members of the company are firmly of the belief that the Bay Horse is destined to become one of the best dividend payers in the State.

The North Star mine, in the Banner district, is showing very rich ore, and good mines are being developed in the Deer Park district. The Gavilan, Pinacate, Cohnilla and Tanquitze districts, will all have new mills by January, 1898, and according to the Riverside Enterprise 100 more stamps will soon be in operation in that county.

———

From the foregoing, it is easily seen that the mining industry throughout Southern California is in an excellent condition. The different lines of railway run in close proximity to a majority of the districts. The stamp mill is fast superceding the arastra. New capital is pouring in to develop prospects, which show pay streaks; improved machinery of all kinds is being bought and placed in position, and with the feeling which now prevails in mining circles, there is no doubt but that the year 1898 will mark an epoch in quartz mining in this section, and that the output of ore will more than double that of any other year.

The above is quite sufficient argument in favor of a general reduction works in Los Angeles.

THE OIL INDUSTRY

OIL of late years has greatly augmented and solidified the wealth of Southern California, and the Secretary of the Produce Oil Exchange furnishes the following commendable article on the subject :

The oil fields of Santa Paula and Puente districts have for years supplied considerable crude petroleum, but not until the discovery of oil in the city of Los Angeles could it be said that Southern California was bountifully supplied with cheap fuel. The comparatively low cost of wells and the accessibility to the market brought the price down to such an extent that today the use of coal or wood for steam and power producing purposes in Southern California has been entirely superceded by oil, and the developments made in the various districts where oil has been found, show that Southern California is richly endowed with oil, and that we are assured of a fuel supply adequate to all demands for years to come. The production of oil has increased as the demand has been created, and from a few hundred barrels a month in the year of 1893, the Los Angeles fields alone are now being called upon for about ninety thousand barrels per month.

There are about five hundred producing wells in this district. Nearly all wells produce during the first ninety days' pumping, fifty per cent. of their entire output for two years, the decline being very rapid after the first three months. The average production of our wells is about six barrels per day, varying from one barrel up.

The oil belt runs almost due east and west and dips to the south; the developments now cover about two miles in length, from three hundred to six hundred feet in width. The western end of the field is badly broken and work in that direction has temporarily ceased. On the eastern end the drillers keep pressing forward with encouraging results. It will soon be necessary to make a long jump, the Catholic cemetery, the Sou'hern Pacific railroad yards, and the river being next in the line of work.

In the work now being done east of the river, results will be watched with great interest by all engaged in the business or use of oil.

The gravity of our oil varies from twelve to nineteen degrees, the lighter oils being mostly from the east end. The heaviest oil comes from the center field, yet one finds both grades of oil from wells within a few hundred feet of each other, the oil from the upper strata being the lighter.

The wells on the north line of the vein reach the oil sand at about seven hundred feet, and at about one thousand feet on the south line; the upper sand varies from forty to one hundred feet; a second sand has been developed at about one hundred feet below the first strata, but in a great many instances, wells have encountered considerable water, after going through the first strata, so as to drown them out. On account of the water no endeavor has so far been made to go deeper than twelve hundred feet.

The base of our oil is asphaltum—it is a safe fuel, its low gravity making it necessary to vaporize it, or heat the oil before it will burn. A small fire could be easily extinguished with the oil at 85 degrees F.

Practical experience has demonstrated that from three to four barrels of oil will do the work of one ton of Australian or Wellington coal. The average price of oil is about one dollar ($1.00) per barrel of 42 gallons.

The Santa Fe R. R. use it extensively on all of their locomotives in Southern California west of Barstow—about forty-five engines. The Southern Pacific have about fifteen engines burning oil, and are constantly changing others. All of our gas and electric plants use it—street cars, laundries, breweries, lime and brick kilns, ice cold storage, etc.

At this writing we are shipping about twenty-five thousand barrels of our product to northern points—mostly to San Francisco, freight rate being fifty-one cents per barrel.

It ought not to be possible to spare any of this fuel for shipment in its crude state. The cheapness of the oil ought to encourage capital to use it in manufacturing.

A refinery on a large scale is wanted; asphaltum and its by-products would pay.

The Santa Fe R. R. developments at Fullerton are proving satisfactory, four wells now being in operation there. The oil is about 20 degrees gravity and the wells produce about the same as an average Los Angeles well.

The Puente field has not been very productive; so far the Puente Company has about forty wells in operation. The last two wells finished by the Puente Company were located by Professor Watts, of the State Geological Department, and results show that science has been triumphant, for the two wells are the largest producers the company has so far developed, and they believe that they have a large area of territory which will produce like results.

A MINIATURE EMPIRE.

MANY principalities, says a late pamphlet issued by the Los Angeles Chamber of Commerce, which have played quite an important part in the political history of Europe, cannot boast half the resources that lie dormant, or only partially developed, within the confines of Los Angeles county

"Los Angeles, while not a very large county, as counties go in the western part of the United States, covers a wide expanse of land, containing about 4000 square miles of territory, being, consequently, almost as large as the State of Connecticut, and twice as large as Delaware. Some four-fifths of the area is capable of cultivation, with water supplied, the remainder being mountainous. The shore line is about eighty five miles in length, the county extending from thirty to fifty miles back from the ocean. Within this area there is a remarkable variety of scenery, soil and climate. There are low, moist valleys, elevated mesas, or table lands, rolling foothills and rugged mountains, some of them snow-capped in winter.

"Some of the most picturesque scenery in the world is found along the foothills of the Sierra Madre range. Especially is this true in the winter season, when the snow-clad mountains form a striking back ground to the wide expanse of dark green orange groves, in which the golden spheres shine out amid the glossy foliage, while the atmosphere is laden with the perfume of myraids of delicate flowers. Higher up, on the summits of these mountains, are groves of noble pine trees, which shade attractive camping grounds for the residents of the plains during the summer months. Then, again, along the seashore, there are breezy stretches of level land, where the temperature varies but a few degrees from January to Christmas.

"The population of Los Angeles county, by the census of 1890, was 101,454. A conservative estimate places the present population of the county at over 175,000. The assessed valuation of property is nearly $100,000,000. The marvelous growth that has been made by this imperial county during the past few years may be seen from the statement that, by the census of 1880, the population was only 33,881, while the assessed valuation, in 1882, was only $20,655,-294.

"A striking evidence of the solid financial condition of Los Angeles county is furnished by the latest statistics of mortgages on real estate in California. In forty-two of the agricultural and commercial counties of California the percentage of loans to the value of property is 19.03 per cent. As the assessed values are not more than two-thirds of the market values of lands and improvements, the actual percentage of indebtedness in the State is only 13.69 per cent, a very low figure. Turning to Los Angeles county, we find that the percentage of mortgage indebtedness amounts to less than 10 per cent, or to be exact, 9.6 per cent."

FOUNDATION PRINCIPLES.

AGRICULTURE, mining, manufacturing and commerce or exchange—these constitute the divisions of human industry, and underneath each are found the ground principles of all successful society. That people are the happiest who most observe the basic elements of human relations and make the least effort to devour one another. As mankind is largely dependent upon what grows out of the earth, agriculture becomes the basis of all efforts to prolong existence. Therefore, he who can best adjust his efforts to those of nature, secures the results. To bring man-force and elementary forces in agriculture into happy union requires thought, study, reflection. In Southern California, brains and muscle meet meritorious nature in thoroughness and attractiveness, soil conditions, meteorological differences, and other influences combine to produce marvels in the interests of the human race, hence Los Angeles is not destined to become alone an aggregation of noted beings but the entire surroundings are fast assuming peculiarities peculiar to the region and the natural attractions. The rural population is tending to density. All the elements of compactness are here, hence the valleys tributary to Los Angeles will ever pour their wealth into her commercial lap. They will not only pour in but also draw out vast quantities of household and agricultural necessities for compensation.

MANUFACTORIES.

There are several hundred factories in successful operation in the city. The Baker Iron Works is a successful enterprise employing a large force of skilled workmen.

The Cudahy Packing Company has stimulated hog raising; and their firm daily uses large numbers of sheep, hogs and cattle. With the facilities to grow swine, the farmers ought to furnish all the hams and bacon required by our people.

There are over three hundred manufactories now in successful operation in this city, and 3000 families are patrons of these home products. With an increased demand for choice articles made at home, our enterprising converters of raw material into usable goods, will find an increased trade, and as this widens every avenue of industry will be stimulated. Let our people stand by the producers.

AMAZING GROWTH.

The eloquence of the recent census cannot be

hushed. Springing from a population of 51,-000 in 1890 to 103,705 in 1897, or a gain of over 100 per cent, is a declaration of growth so emphatic that the dullest can comprehend. A spirit of contentment prevails, and the pleasures which flow from all the genial natural elements are sure to win many more ten thousands who shall become weary of nature's variableness where they now are.

ASPHALTUM.

In and near the city are large beds of brea or bitumen from which is manufactured an excellent article of asphaltum for street paving and roofing purposes. It is found to possess superior qualities in the construction of lemon curing houses or any structure requiring an even temperature, since it is almost impervious to heat. As the necessity for packing houses and dairies increase, the demand for this cheap, reliable and lasting material will increase, thus extending its manufacture. The bitumen and oil products for the past year exceed $1,000,000. Mr. A. W. Ludlow says this industry is in its infancy and the future development of it will some day surprise the world.

BUILDINGS.

The accretions and developments during the past three years have been marvelous, based, as they have been, on sound financial principles. Over $10,000,000 have been spent here on public and private buildings and improvements. Many of the business edifices and residences would be considered ornaments in cities with five times the population. The architecture is varied. The monotony of sameness is absent, thus giving relief to the eye, or rather conveying rapture to the artistic mind. This upward and onward stride is simply another proof of the unsurpassed soil, locative and climatic conditions, and as capital shall move and understand this inviting field, new industries will spring up, calling for many additional magnificent structures.

The following table will show the developments in building from July, 1889, to December 1st, 1897:

July, 1889, to Dec. 1st, 1889, 194 permits to cost.....................$ 797,121
1889-90, 746 permits, to cost........   1,146,851
1890-91, 656 permits, to cost........   1,306,130
1891-92, 789 permits, to cost........   1,888,000
1892-93, 1312 permits, to cost........   1,639,000
1893-94, 1795 permits, to cost........   2,326,000
1894-95, 2415 permits, to cost........   3,885,883
1895-96, 2312 permits, to cost........   2,751,630
1896-97, 2015 permits, to cost........   2,481,685

Total.... ....$18,222,500

THE PUBLIC LIBRARY.

A reading people are a thinking people, a full people; abreast of the indomitable pluck and perseverance of our cousins to the north and to the east, our public library, evolving out of small beginnings, has grown, not to the full stature of manhood, but to handsome, vigorous youth-hood, filled with an animation which bespeaks high attainments in the nearby.

HOMES.

The fame of this climate has swept the horizon of our eastern neighbors and penetrated the living masses of the European continent. All attempts to shake off these genial conditions, where earth, air, sunshine and water joins hands in one continuous round of fructiferous delights, are so many failures. Once panoplied with nature's charms and drinking in her pure and unsullied favors, the "tourist" as well as the homeseeker and "homesicker," are impelled to enjoy those natural fascinations in due time by living in them; hence Southern California will ever be the one free spot where the lover of nature's undisturbed harmonies will offer for him the largest possibilities of paradisical realization on earth. Our homes, therefore, are designed, in the very nature of the circumstances, to become the admiration of the acutest esthetic and the commendation of a growing civilization.

Given limitless, natural possibilities, our homes may present the attractiveness of an Eden. The unending round of variety of flowers, the diversity of shrubbery, the helpfulness of the artist—all combine to develop the most charming places of quietude and restfulness. Many such are already ornamenting the lovely city, which sits at the foot of the Sierra Madre, looking out on yonder placid water, destined to cast into her lap a magnificent commerce.

SAVINGS.

The greater and simpler the facilities for laborers and artisans to place their surplus earnings, be they ever so small, in places of safety, the greater the prosperity of the entire community; for a people who save with the view of securing homes are not likely to be otherwise than contented as well as useful. The September, 1897, report of five of our savings banks show deposits of $4,022,532.12. The deposits in other banks bring this sum up to over $12,000,000. To this should be added the millions which go into building associations from parties, who would, without this means of applying their surplus toward the payment of homes, perhaps permit it to go in luxuries and dainties.

OUTSIDE RESOURCES.

LOS ANGELES, like all other progressive cities, is not wholly dependent for extension upon the resources within her limits. Domestic trade relations are fixed upon established commercial law—supply and demand. The inherent forces of a city are stimulated largely by exchange. The incoming and outgoing necessities and luxuries through the arteries of trade, like healthful blood coursing through the human system, replenish and strengthen the body politic. The more trade the greater the strength. Los Angeles accretes through the tremendous outside helps by land and by sea.

In matters of horticulture the 11,000 car loads of oranges and lemons during the year 1887, the 600 carloads of English walnuts, the 30,000,000 pounds of sugar, the products of 1,300 quince trees, 38,000 plums, 974,000 French prunes, 75,000 other prunes, 71,000 figs, 237,000 apples, 23,000 cherries, 1,005,000 peaches, and 1,075,000 apricots, millions of pounds of strawberries and blackberries, a hundred thousand tons of hay, train loads of potatoes, and 600 cars of celery, together with a long list of other vegetables and cereals, are important factors in our city's development.

The production of string beans, green peas, chili peppers and tomatoes, for winter shipment to supply trade demands north and east, is an inviting field. Capital may find here remunerative investment and an extension of the present efforts in frostless locations. Potatoes, cabbage, onions and cauliflower are exported in large quantities.

The following will show how our citizens may indulge in ripe fruits every day in the year:

Oranges .... All the year
Lemons .... All the year
Limes .... All the year

Figs	July to Christmas
Almonds	October
Apples	July to November
Pears	July to November
Grapes	July to December
Peaches	June to Christmas
Apricots	June to September
Plums and prunes	June to September
Japanese persimmons	Nov. and Dec.
Guavas	Nearly all the year
Loquats	May and June
Strawberries	Nearly all the year
Raspberries	June to September
Blackberries	June to September
Currants	May and June
Watermelons	July to December
Cantaloupes	July to December
Mulberries	July to December
Nectarines	August
Olives	December and January
Pomegranates	September and December
Quinces	October and December

HAY AND GRAINS.

When the existing conditions relative to horticultural productions and the requirements of cities and towns and mines are taken into consideration, the importance of general farming as a feeder to the southwest metropolis assumes gratifying proportions. The majority of fruit growers are hay and grain purchasers. Those in towns and cities who own a cow or horse, together with livery stables and public institutions, are patrons of the farmer. Large quantities of hay are sent to the mines where domestic animals are used. The amount passing through the hands of the dealers aggregates many tens of thousands of tons annually.

DAIRYING.

As the fruit growers depend upon the farmer for his hay and grain, and the grain mower looks to the fruit grower for his fruits, so does the horticulturist in a measure trade with the dairyman for his milk and butter, and the dairyman seeks the horticulturist for fruits and nuts. The reciprocal relations between producers in Southern California are manifold, each occupying his distinct field. This kind of reciprocity calls not for acute diplomacy on the part of students of economy, but the necessities of mutual dependence are the arbiters of all claims.

The growing of alfalfa on low lands and its rapid growth enabling its owners to cut from six to twelve tons per acre during summer, is the secret of the appearance of the fine butter found in our markets. Gratifying as has been the development of dairying the past few years, the surprising growth of cities and country beckon capitalists to the extension of cheese and butter making.

POULTRY AND EGGS.

Notwithstanding the attempts of ranchers and specialists to meet the demand for eggs and poultry, we have to import millions of pounds from the East. Persons with little money and an abundance of pluck and energy may find many little niches in the country where domestic fowls can be raised with profit.

HONEY.

California honey is celebrated, even finding a market in Europe. The hills and vales abound with flowers laden with that which causes the bee to search them with diligence. Five million pounds of honey are exported annually. Men of moderate means find this an inviting calling, and our city realizes the value of the honey trade. The sugar beet and honey bee are a unit in their sweet endeavors. In this, as in all other efforts to provide for man's inner needs, the country around Los Angeles is lavishly willing and abundantly able.

SARDINES.

A firm at San Pedro employs seventy-five men canning sardines. The quality of the canned article is equal to that put up in foreign countries. The city receives its share of benefit from this new industry.

THE OLIVE INDUSTRY.

Great strides have have been made in olive culture the past few years. More than fifty varieties are now grown, and the superior quality of the pickled olive and oil are rapidly working their way into favorable markets. The supply is not equal to the demand, and the beautiful hills which rise throughout the valleys invite capitalists to adorn them with this elegant evergreen that is sure to return a handsome revenue for the investment. The hills thus ornamented would set our country far in advance of Palestine in the zenith of her splendor, besides producing an income which would support thousands of people. The world is the market for California's delicious, pickled olives.

ELECTRIC LIGHT AND POWER.

The development of electric light and power by means of water power in the mountains, doubtless will open the way for cheap power for small factories. There are many useful articles which might be manufactured in this city, and no doubt will be so soon as the needful power can be supplied. Capitalists are busy along these lines in the San Gabriel and Santa Ana rivers, and the day is near at hand when these developments will give our city a new impetus in the direction of manufacturing.

SOME NEEDFUL THINGS.

One million pair of shoes are bought annually in Southern California. The hides of our beeves and pelts of our sheep are sent back east, to be tanned with eastern bark, made into shoes by eastern workmen, and then freighted back here for our own feet. Two freights, several manufactories, a half-dozen or more profits—all of which our people could have and should have. We are growing the canaigre which will give us the tannic acid to fit the hides for the shoemaker. The shoemaker will eat our fruit, poultry, eggs, fish, flour and vegetables. He will buy a lot and build thereon, thus stimulating the lumber trade, the hardware business, the lime and glass and paint industries, and many other lines of commerce.

The wool we send east should be kept here and made into clothing and blankets. The electric power can turn the spindles; the tailors can turn out the suits and in this way every legitimate avenue of trade will receive such momentum that our city will soon double her wealth and population.

The corn necessary for canning can be grown on our rich soil, and thus we need not send cash to Maine for all of this product. With our unrivaled fruits, we should manufacture our jams, jellies and preserves, sugar being made in the very center of this fruit area. More hogs should be raised to stimulate the raising of more corn and alfalfa, and the curing of bacon. More tomato canneries, and factories to make extracts, and vinegar from orange culls, are inviting men of means and brains to be useful.

And the miner needs mills and smelters to work his ores. Thousands of square miles of rich mineral land lies contiguous to Los Angeles, and with the cheap fuel and power at hand, a fair portion of the reduction of ores ought to come here.

BRUSH, PENCIL, CAMERA.

Though time and elements may cause erosions

and physical changes, the undulating mountains, the grand cañons, the perspective and variegated foothills, the sunlitten and rainbowed falls, the enchanted landmarks of a people going out, the unrivalled green and orange and olive mingling in the orchards, are likely to remain and delight the eye of the artist and plethorize his purse. A gentleness and loveliness so perfectly characterizes the scenery in and around our city that the knights of brush and camera fail not to appreciate their golden opportunities. This everlasting brilliancy of sky, islands, hills, vales, mountains and rural perfections makes the true artist wear his heart all over his face. California scenery cannot be described. It may be praised. Language cannot convey the sublimity which Deity heaped up here. The artist tries to copy it. Sometimes he nearly succeeds; more frequently his failure is his greatest success. Still, nature's scenery never tires in being practiced on.

WOMAN'S CHRISTIAN TEMPERANCE UNION

THE Woman's Christian Temperance Union invaded Southern California in March, 1883, by the organization of a Union at Santa Barbara. At Los Angeles it gained a home in April following, and by September, 1883, thirteen Unions were ready to join hands—most, if not all of them, the children of Miss Frances E. Willard, National President.

During her visit to the Pacific Coast, Miss Willard saw the need of a division of the State for effectual temperance work, and through her efforts two State organizations were formed. The seven southern counties united to create the Woman's Christian Temperance Union of Southern California at a State Convention held in the First Presbyterian Church, Los Angeles, Sept. 20th, 1883, when Miss Martha N. Hathaway of Los Angeles, was elected President.

One year later the President pro tem of Kern county, said in her annual report: "This county has no Unions, and has never been visited by any W. C. T. U. workers. Kern county is larger than the State of Vermont, and has only one church building, two ministers of the M. E. church, and one appointment filled twice a month by an Episcopal minister from Fresno." Through such difficult surroundings has the work pressed forward until all of the counties were organized for temperance work.

In one year the "lucky thirteen" charter Unions doubled their number and had a membership of 632. That number has increased until now there are 88 Woman's Christian Temperance Unions, and 13 Young Woman's Christian Temperance Unions, with 1600 active and 264 honorary members.

The State officers are: President, Mrs. Mary A. Kenney; Vice-President, Mrs. S. Ogilvie Webber; Corresponding Secretary, Miss G. T. Stickney; Recording Secretary, Mrs. Lizzie H. Mills; Assistant Recording Secretary, Mrs. Sophia Wood Plimpton. The State motto is, "The battle is not yours, but God," and from the first the evangelistic department has been the foundation of all the work, and Christ Jesus the chief corner stone.

Petition and legislative work were among the first efforts, in which co-operation was had with Northern California white ribboners. Through the combined efforts the "age of consent" for girls has been raised from ten to sixteen years, though eighteen was desired; a law compelling scientific temperance instruction in the public schools was secured; one forbidding the sale of liquor and tobacco to minors under sixteen years of age, and in 1892 a bill passed granting school suffrage to women, only to meet a pocket veto. The faithfulness of the State Superintendent of penal work culminated in the establishing of the

Whittier Reform School for boys and girls, which is now under State control, and doing much good.

Forty-two departments of work are operated, being grouped under the general heads of Organization, Preventative, Educational, Social and Legal. There is hardly a cry of distress from humanity but what finds a sympathetic response of practical help from white ribboners. From protecting the purity of childhood to rescuing the mother's wayward boy or girl, in prison or out, the W. C. T. U. seeks to establish the "white life for two."

From a half belief in the high license of the liquor traffic, the opinions of the white-ribboners firmly favor prohibition. From a fear of endorsing woman suffrage an advance has been made until the woman who disfavors the movement is the exception.

In 1892 Southern California W. C. T. U. was asked to, and did, adopt the Ransom Industrial Home—a home in Los Angeles for friendless and erring women—which had been established and conducted by Los Angeles ladies. Since that time many women have found a temporary shelter there, and others, the first real christian home and care they ever knew. With few exceptions the wayward girl's have gone out from the Home to lead honest, pure lives. It is almost entirely supported by free will offerings.

A central attraction now is Temperance Temple in Los Angeles, the lot for which was donated to the society by the Good Templars, and upon which now stands a four-story, brick and stone building, which cost nearly $50,000, being architecturally the nicest building in the city at that time. A large auditorium and State headquarters occupy the first floor, while above are nicely finished rooms for offices or lodging-rooms.

Of the seven Presidents who have presided over the State Union, two are "resting from their labors, and their works do follow them"—Mrs. Olive B. Bird, the third President, and Mrs. Sophia A. Keyes, the sixth. The others of the seven are Miss Martha N. Hathaway, Mrs. Lucy D. More, Mrs. N. P. J. Button, Mrs. Mary E. Garbutt, and present incumbent, Mrs. Mary A. Kenney.

As the little bow of white ribbon is the badge of the society, so the women of this southland named their official organ the Southern California White Ribbon. It was founded in 1889 by Mrs. Mary Case Lord, who for four years was its talented editor. Mrs. Anna S. Wolfskill is the present able editor and manager, and she, like all her predecessors, serves gratuitously.

INTERVIEWS, ETC.

WE find a diversity of opinion among the business men in regard to more factories being established in our midst. Some disagree with us but the majority seem to think it entirely feasible to establish new manufacturing industries in Los Angeles. As Mr. Warren Gillelen says: "A more diversified system of manufacturing might be profitably engaged in in Los Angeles—with ample capital and wise management at the head."

We believe there is an opening here for the manufacture of eucalyptus, even if the timber must be cultivated. In this connection General E. P. Johnson says: "I don't believe it is a practical proposition, though I am willing to admit that eucalyptus is a hard wood and susceptible of a fine polish, etc., but we haven't the timber in sufficient quantities and the average tree isn't large enough." All due respect to the General's opinion; still we invite discussion on this subject as we believe there is a field here for that branch of industry.

As to glass: Mr. Victor Ponet is sanguine capital could find no better opening anywhere than in Los Angeles in a well appointed and properly managed glass works. We agree with the gentleman, if fuel is cheap enough, as that is the great desideratum in the manufacture of glass. If we are correctly informed it requires three carloads of bituminous coal to manufacture one carload of sand into glass. Our oil for fuel will, or has, doubtless solved that question.

We don't care to discuss the factories which we think might be established in Los Angeles, but we feel sanguine that when practical men, seeking new fields for investment, learn of the openings here they will not be slow in taking advantage of it. And in this connection it is within the bounds of truth to say that more capital will seek investment west, in 1898, than ever in the history of the commercial world.

In speaking of the opening in Los Angeles for a power house—i.e. a building provided with power, heat, shafting, etc., to be subject to small manufacturers—Mr. F. W. King says: "I agree with you on that proposition, as I was in a building like that back east and thirty factories were in operation under one roof." As to other branches Mr. K. said: "I know we are manufacturing in a small way and will continue to enlarge as the country develops and I see no reason why more factories might not be established here with every prospect of success."

Bishop George Montgomery thinks our city is on the eve of prosperity and that capital will soon be attracted and invested in a more diversified system of manufacturing in our growing and lovely city.

Wm. F. Bosbyshell says: "I haven't time for

an interview, but I sincerely believe this is the best place in the United States for a smelter or general reduction works."

Thos. Pascoe says: "Of course I can't speak of manufacturing as well as some others in the city, but I know there is much more now being done in manufacturing than most of our people realize. I think it is entirely feasible to talk of more factories in Los Angeles and I don't see why a glass works wouldn't prove a profitable industry."

Mr. S. B. Lewis says: "Of course manufacturing will pay in Los Angeles, but I am decidedly more in favor of urging small factories. I would rather see fifty small concerns, each employing ten, than one big factory working five hundred men, as the small ones will develop with the country and be a big success provided practical men are at the head."

E. F. C. Klokke says: "I don't feel competent to discuss the question of more factories, but you can put me down as being always in favor of any and everything to advance the best interests of our city. In this connection I want you to see Prof. Woodbridge and have him prepare you an article on the opening here for capital in manufacturing our offal fruit (lemons) up into acids."

General C. F. A. Last: "Too busy for an interview, but I believe there is a big field, and a profitable one, too, in Los Angeles for more factories."

The General's partner in the oil business,

Joseph Baer, says: "The cheap oil for fuel has solved the question of manufacturing in our city, and I expect to see them develop rapidly."

Mr. M. A. Hamburger says: "Of course manufacturing here will pay and is paying. We are compelled to enlarge our manufacturing plant and the belt works here, also a necktie factory and several others are increasing rapidly. This belt factory we buy from largely as they make a better belt and and more suited to this trade than any eastern concern." The gentleman thought great strides in manufacturing would be made in the next five years.

Mr. Bluett says: "I am an enthusiast over manufacturing being profitably engaged in in Los Angeles, and I believe the development of manufactories in our city in the next five years will surprise everybody. That's all I have to say, sir."

∴ ∴ ∴

"Los Angeles and Southern California, as Viewed by a Life Underwriter," is the subject of this article. As the modern history of this section dates back about ten years, I will confine myself to this period. While "life" business was, of course, done previous to that time, it is only during the above period hat Los Angeles has become the Southern California headquarters for all the leading companies of the country. The life business, like all other branches, has become a great deal more conservative in recent years, i. e., while a large volume of business was written during the "boom," it was, after all, only "boom business," and very little of it now remains on the companies' books. In fact, only a small proportion ever paid a second annual premium. All this has changed much in recent years. The business done today is indicative of the stability and prosperity of the people of Southern California, just as the boom business was indicative of the general unrest, "the here-today-and-there-tomorrow" feeling, and the financial unrest—aimless and speculative spirit of the days of '86 and '87. The business written in the last four or five years is being renewed at a ratio of 3 to 1, as compared to the business of ten years ago, showing that the people are more settled, their incomes more regular, and that obligations incurred are met, and that deliberation has taken the place of the erstwhile blind haste and chase after phantom fortune.

The personnel of the "field men" has improved in the same ratio. Where formerly the chain-lightning and plug hat and kid-gloved solicitor made his rounds, getting applications, no matter by what representations, the successful life insurance man of today must have not only standing in the community, but a thorough knowledge of the business, and last, but not least, a good contract for sale.

As there is no rule without an exception, so the above statement needs modification in at least one particular. I refer to the many local assessment life associations, whose only claim for business is "cheapness," and occasionally the names of some more or less prominent men on the Board of Directors, who rarely ever know even the A, B, C of the science of life insurance. Of course, the rule of the "survival of the fittest," will, in course of time, clear the field of these mathematical impossibilities; unfortunately at the cost of a great many of the good people of this section. We are after all only in a transitory stage, both commercially and socially, and must pass through the regular course of evolution. A really good thing will always have quack imitators anywhere, but a comparatively new territory like ours offers a particularly fertile soil for all sorts of wild cat schemes until the people here as elsewhere shall have learned that good insurance, like any other first-class article of merchandise, costs money and cannot be had for nothing.

In conclusion let me say, that for legitimate life underwriting, there is no better field on the coast than Southern California.

E. C. SCHNABEL.

We have several opera houses, music halls, etc., and when asked how Los Angeles compared with other cities as an amusement loving city, Mr. H. C. Wyatt said: "In answering your question as to the merits of Los Angeles as a 'show town,' will say there are few cities in the United States of its size which is better. Our patrons are very particular and want the best; can't gull them with cheap attractions, they come very nearly knowing what is good, or rather what they want. Price makes no difference if the attraction suits them, and if they are not suited a cut in prices will not draw them out. At present we have three regular theaters; one playing only first-class attractions, one as a rule plays stock companies and one a vaudeville theater. Our theaters run the entire year and there are several music halls also which run every night—but with all this I assure you all are doing well. I am also quite certain that we will do even better in the future."

Mr. H. F. Chase says: "I am enthusiastic on the subject of manufacturing and fully believe that well directed energy and harmonious effort on the part of our people will result in building up a more diversified system of manufacturing in Los Angeles."

Mr. Chase was asked how our hotels compared with other cities and replied that no city the size of Los Angeles could compare with it not only in numbers but in the efficient management, excellent cusine, high character of the chefs and extra service throughout. He also spoke in quite flattering terms of our many delightful resort hotels and predicted a profitable business for all the coming season.

Mr. R. W. Burnham furnishes the following:

"The advantage of manufactures over agriculture as a source of national wealth lies in the making possible a denser population and opening a more promptly extensible field to enterprise. In the history of the development of different sections of the civilized world this fact is shown indisputably, that a progressive community cannot long continue to have its whole practical life founded on territorial property. It must sieze and hold every opportunity to extend its commercial and manufacturing interests, or it will soon be distanced in the race for supremacy.

"Time was when Southern California felt that all prosperity petitions must be made to the goddess of the bountiful harvest; that the wealth of this section lay entirely in horticultural and agricultural resources; and that her manufactures (properly speaking, not manufactures at all) must be confined to the conversion of articles of food into a more suitable and convenient form for shipment. But the discovery and development of her petroleum fields providing a fuel for manufacturing purposes, equivalent to coal at $3.50 a ton, necessarily expanded her industrial possibilities. Raw material seeks the cheap motive power. 'The mountain cannot go to Mahomet, Mahomet goes to the mountain.' New England built her great factories on her water courses, brought her cotton from the south, her wool from the west, and her great textile industries grew. Pennsylvania had her wealth of coal for a basis, Ohio her natural gas. Southern California has her petroleum, not to mention the water powers of her mountain streams, already being utilized and converted into electricity for use on the plains below. Additional encouragements to ambitious plans, directed toward the making of this section a hive of industrial activities, are offered by a mild climate demanding inexpensive buildings, labor plentiful, living cheap, and lastly, an abundance of two important raw materials, wool and iron.

"I feel justified in saying that an investor can place his money here in many lines of manufactures with a reasonable promise of a fair return, if only desirous of capturing the home market, a few lines hold the prospect of successful competition with eastern centers.

"The success of our beet sugar factories makes one note that as $120,000,000 is annually sent from the United States for foreign sugar this field is hardly crowded as yet.

"The extensive raising of canaigre suggests mills for the extraction of tannin, boot and shoe factories, tanneries, etc. Large quantities of raw hides are now sent to the east each year to be re-imported in various forms of merchandise.

"The wool industry is reviving, and under tariff protection should increase fast. It has been one California's greatest productions. Millions of pounds are shipped to the east to be manufactured into dress goods, woolen hosiery, knitted underwear, blankets, flannels, etc., and sent back to . .s coast for consumption. All these can be turned out here at less than eastern manufacturers prices.

"As yet coke is a necessity in rendering iron

ores available for commercial purposes, and until the Salt Lake road taps for us the coal fields of Southern Utah and makes possible the establishment of reduction works, our inexhaustible bodies of iron ore must remain unappropriated virgin wealth and our dollars go to swell the coffers of eastern and European dealers in manufactured and pig iron.

"I say nothing of the making of agricultural implements, or the undoubted room for expansion in more varied manufactures from our horticultural products; the soundness of investment along these lines is undisputed.

"Lord Bacon says there are three things which make a community great and prosperous: fertile soil, busy workshops, and easy conveyance for men and goods from place to place. The fertile soil is beyond dissent; the certainty of a deep water harbor guarantees us transportation facilities as the need arises, and our cheap motive power and abundance of raw material, holds the great industrial possibilities needed for the third side of this magic triangle that encompasses wealth and power. But these possibilities will not materialize into actualities without the dynamo power of human mind and skill. Men of enterprise with faith in our manifest destiny must light the furnaces. Our people must be enthused to the point of feeling a sectional pride in keeping the wheels moving of every new industry established."

It is surprising the number of young men in

business in Los Angeles—young men at the head of our institutions—and on this subject Mr. Isadore B. Dockweiler says: "There's no city in any country on earth where the young men are so much in the front as right in Los Angeles. They are at the head of most of our financial institutions, and all lines of mercantile pursuits and the vast majority of our able professional men are young men, or at most just bordering on middle age; and you can't find a more progressive, energetic and higher class of men from a brainy standpoint anywhere."

Mr. Wm. Workman predicts an era of wonderful growth and development in the manufacture of iron and steel when the new road is completed to Salt Lake City. He says the world will be surprised at our progress when these vast deposits of iron are made accessible by rail from Los Angeles, and that he expects to see this city one of the iron and steel marts of the United States soon after the completion of the new railroad.

SENATOR WHITE'S SUMMING UP.

Senator White contributes the following to "The Great West:"

"Southern California has advanced in a very remarkable manner during the last twenty years. The center of the greatest progress is undoubtedly Los Angeles city, but the increase of wealth and population has been general Notwithstanding the almost unique prosperity of this section, the want of a deep water harbor, safe at all seasons, has been recognized as a serious drawback. Indeed, it has been universally conceded that the further advance of this part of the country must be considerably retarded unless congress grants aid through the appropriation bills. The vast mountain range separating Southern California and also Arizona from Central and Northern California has increased the embarrassment by rendering transportation more difficult and expensive. While deep sea vessels now anchor at San Pedro, Redondo and Port Los Angeles, such anchorage cannot be deemed absolutely reliable in tempestuous weather, and this truth is manifest in marine insurance rates. A casual examination of these facts indicates some of the consequences of the construction of a commodious and thoroughly protected harbor. In the first place, freight reductions would be had. There will be increased water carriage. This will lead to manufacturing and growing commerce. The population immediately tributary to San Pedro consists of over two hundred thousand people, to say nothing of Arizona, and must be added to day by day. A correspondingly augmented and diversified business be will disclosed, attended by all the enterprise through which wealth seeks investment. Hitherto all efforts to induce direct trade from the Orient with the southwest have failed mainly because of want of harbor facilities. The shortest all-rail route across the United States will be found in the Southern Pacific line from San Pedro to Galveston, and when the harbor improvements are completed there is no doubt that a large amount of through freight will be transported over this route.

"Looking further into the future and contemplating the completion of the Nicaraugua canal, we find in the trade development incident to that great work another reason for pleasurable anticipations.

"While mining matters in Arizona have been considered of less moment than formerly, still there is much going on in that territory. The rich country in the neighborhood of Phoenix is prolific in agricultural wealth. Fruit matures much earlier than in any other locality. The new harbor will be needed more and more, and will be the outlet and freight rate regulator for an immense area. Incidentally, the benefits to result from the San Pedro harbor work will be felt throughout California, and will extend to Salt Lake and St. Louis. It is very satisfactory to know that when this work is done it will have been accomplished in spite of selfish obstruction, and in the face of powerful influences antagonistic to the public."

Mr. Wm. Geo. Blewett furnishes the following readable and interesting article:

"Beautiful for situation is Los Augeles. Between the mountains and the sea she stands flooded with sunshine, yet cool in the shade of magnificent foliage, while bedecked with flowers and crowned with orange blossoms, like a fair young bride.

"In the days of old, when her sons and daughters dreamed of poetry—not of prose—and betook themselves to thinking more of beauty and repose than of business cares and worry, she was named 'The City of the Angeles.' Well did she deserve the honor. And today, while the poetical gives place to the practical, and up-to-date enterprise takes the place of the 'ease of the ancients,' still she stands a 'thing of beauty and a joy forever.' And while 'Home, Sweet Home," has charms that nothing on earth possesses, just so long will the 'City of Homes' be the central gem in this land of golden promise.

"No one factor has been more potent in producing this city of cozy homes, where the wage-earners can literally sit under the shade of their own vines and fig trees, than her seventeen mutual building and loan associations. The purposes of these associations, which in their general features are similar to co-operative banks of New England, and the great Berbeck Society of Great Britain, is to assist persons of little or no means to obtain homes. Those that are blessed with wealth will of course come and build beautiful mansions in the valley and on the hilltop and bask in the sunshine, while they add a long lease to life and climatic comforts to old age. But what of the frugal and the thrifty, those with more muscle than means; the honest toiler, the backbone of every community—how shall he be able to say 'I live here, my home is here, and this is my abiding place forever?' He cannot attain such comforts unaided. He must be helped. The Mutual Building Association is the chief means to that end. Only the citizen that owns his home can honestly say 'Home and country are one to me—they stand or fall together.' Let it here be said to the credit of the Mutual Building Associations that no portion of the citizenship in Los Angeles more fully appreciates the comforts of home, and the power for good behind the home, where the loved ones are sheltered, than our wage-earners that have secured their homes through the aid offered by these co-operative societies. Then it is, when so precisely obtained, that the home is the safeguard and bulwark of American liberty. There are thousands of homes in Los Angeles, owned by their occupants, and built through these mutual associations that would never be otherwise built, because upon this kind of 'purchase plan' the payments are made monthly and for about the same amount as the rent would otherwise be. So it is that in the space of 72 to 84 or 100 months, according to the amount so paid monthly, these homes have been paid for. They stand today free from debt, monuments of beauty to the credit of the thoughtful, persevering, frugal wage-earners of this city, whose honest labor has thus been made to adorn many of its streets with the most inviting beauty; where the birds and flowers mingle, and the merry children prattle, and the boys and girls are dancing to the music of content, with books and pleasure plenty, while the mothers smile all sweetness and the fathers are at peace, feeling they have done their duty both to loved ones and to the country.

"The plan is simple. If the wage-earner has nothing to begin with but labor, he can at any time combine with it 'frugality,' which enables him to save his money by taking 'deposit stock,' then, after 12, 20 or 30 months, suppose his monthly deposits amount to $500, he may then withdraw this sum and buy a lot, and upon it and the $800, five-room cottage he plans to build he may borrow the $800, which is then paid out to him by the Association, as the building progresses. Finally it is completed and he occupies it. He repays the sum by taking 8 shares in the Association, of the par value of $100 each, and pays therefor 70c each per month, i.e. $4.80. This is a sinking fund that the borrower is creating monthly, which, with his pro rata share of the profit, matures his stock to par in about 96 months, and it being then worth $800, his loan is thus repaid in full. It will be observed that only $460.80 has been deposited to mature $800, hence $339.20 of profit is realized as the borrower's share. The usual rate of interest paid is six per cent., and a premium of 50 cents per share per month for priority of loan, making one per cent., or $1 per month for each $100; hence the monthly payment for above named $800 would be $12.80, just about the rent charged for a similar cottage. The renter would have only 96 receipts to show, while the borrower would have his home paid for.

"There are in the State of California 155 of these Mutual Building and Loan Associations with an authorized capital stock of nearly $700,000,000 and a working capital paid in of nearly $22,000,000. For the fiscal year of '96 '97, they made net profits of $1,337,824.42, or an average of about 7 1-5 per cent. on the loans in force. The associations in this State are divided into three classes. First.—"Locals," that operate in the immediate locality in which (see Cal. '97 Report) organized, and they made a net profit last year of $6\frac{3}{4}$ per cent. Second.—"Nationals" that operate all over the State, and they made a net profit of $11\frac{1}{4}$ per cent. Third.—"The Co-operative Banks," a combination of banking and building loan, operating throughout the State, made a net profit of 6 57-100 per cent. The national plan is by far the most successful, both in the way of profits, and in the number of dwellings erected in proportion to the money invested. These associations were first organized in this State in 1872. For the first ten years the busines was small, but during the last fifteen years, and especially so within the last five years, it has been very large. Some 12,000 homes have been built altogether that probably house 60,000 people. It is but fair to presume that fully 75 per cent. of this number would not otherwise have obtained a home, hence about 45,000 to 50,000 people are today comfortably situated in their own homes in California, by and through this mutual system of home getting that would still be an "unknown quantity" of no fixed benefit to any community. Of the good done by these associations, the half will never be told. It means to the State a better citizenship, and to the respective localities a greater degree of prosperity than if this accumulated wealth was otherwise distributed. It is now a part of the State's material wealth, but under a lesser home influence on the part of the people, it would be tied up in landlordism, too much of which is a curse. It is estimated that in Los Angeles alone, about 75 per cent. of the property owners owing homes that cost $500 to $5000 each, have built on this monthly payment installment plan; hence the material thus used and the labor performed kept our fair city alive with the music of "hammer and saw" through the past four years, when other cities saw but little or no sign of progress. The natural resources of Southern California, both in soil and climate, cannot help but make Los Angeles a great metropolis, and these Mutual Building and Loan Associations are the very best systems extant for enabling the wage-earner to save and build for himself a home, and will do more toward helping the new-comer to become "a settler for good" than perhaps any other one factor, by simply helping the willing and the thrifty to help themselves.

www.ingramcontent.com/pod-product-compliance
Lightning Source LLC
Chambersburg PA
CBHW032228230426
43666CB00033B/1632